RUBBING CRAFT

RUBBING CRAFT

How to rub doors, letterboxes, gravestones, manhole covers and how to use these designs to make jewelry, T-shirts, needlepoint and more.

by Cecily Barth Firestein

QUICK FOX

New York London

To my bemused husband for his complete support and encouragement, and to my bemused friend Claire Dunphy, who launched the "Rubbing Queen" on her adventure, and to Ellen Stern, who pointed to the right direction.

International Standard Book Number: 0-8256-3062-2
Library of Congress Catalog Card Number: 76-56570
Printed in the United States of America.

In Great Britain: Book Sales Ltd., 78 Newman Street, London W1, England.
In Canada: Gage Trade Publishing, P.O. Box 5000, 164 Commander Blvd., Agincourt, Ontario M1S 3C7.

Book and cover design by Jean Callan King/Visuality
Illustrations by Lily Hou
Photographs by Alain Jullien
Cover photos by Herb Wise, taken at The Waldorf-Astoria Hotel.
Woven art photos, p. 91, by Mike Wulfman

Rubbing from west wall of the temple at Angkor Wat, Cambodia, done with earth pigments and oil.

Frontispiece: Rubbing done with graphite at the American Museum of Natural History.

Foreword

In our mechanized and sophisticated society today, it may seem inexplicable that there has suddenly grown up such an intense interest in rubbings. Possibly one of the main reasons is that it is an art technique within the manual dexterity of all of us, and the subjects rubbed are quite often works of art of a highly decorative nature from a bygone nostalgic age. The rubbings themselves are excellent documentations of architectural details, tombstones, industrial decorative patterns, and archaeological carvings. The originals from which the rubbings have been made are often parts of buildings or fragmentary stone carvings in remote locations or objects of such size and weight that a private person cannot collect them. In many cases, it would not be feasible or even proper for a museum to own the original works. For that reason, the major museums of America, including the Museum of the City of New York, collect rubbings as documentary evidence, and in some cases, the rubbings are actually superior to photographs, particularly in very low reliefs which may have suffered from exposure to the elements.

Rubbings also can be considered as art objects themselves. The keen eye of the rubber has selected the precise detail he or she wished to isolate and record by means of this engrossing technique. Private collectors often decorate the walls of their homes with a variety of highly personal choices of rubbings which they have made themselves. It is an extremely gratifying method of self-expression, and the final results are not only handsome but useful as well. Indeed, highly sophisticated silhouette patterns created by rubbing lend themselves to utilization by designers in many ways such as for textile designs and wallpaper.

As I write these words of introduction to this valuable book at home in my library, the walls around me are covered with rubbings from the great architectural monument, Angkor Wat. What would we now give for the documentation of the great temples of Greece or Rome, Mesopotamia and Egypt, had rubbings from their facades survived to today. It may well be that contemporary rubbers are doing a great service for humanity by helping to document and record our civilization.

While we all may enjoy the hobby of rubbings, certainly artistic talent is an asset. In this regard, we are most fortunate that the artist, Cecily Firestein, some years ago became enamored with this engaging subject. Out of her experience, experimentation, and practical approaches, she has systemized everything you have ever wanted to know about rubbings and were afraid to ask. This practical book is a welcome step forward in this age-old art.

Joseph Veach Noble
Director
Museum of the City of New York

Contents

Graphite rubbing of turn-of-the-century raised wallpaper from Central Synagogue, N.Y.C.

Foreword *5*
Preface *7*
Introduction *10*

PART 1
A BRIEF HISTORY OF RUBBING *13*

PART 2
LIFTING RUBBINGS: MATERIALS AND METHODS *19*
Materials *21*
Methods *26*
Reproducing Your Rubbing *44*
Storage and Display of Rubbings *44*
Sources and Supplies *46*

PART 3
PROJECTS *51*
Linocuts *52*
Woodworking *56*
Appliqué *62*
Hand Embroidery *64*
Machine Embroidery *66*
Doll or Pillow *68*
Needlepoint *70*
Latch Hooking *72*
Stencils and Silkscreens *74*
Photographic Color Transfers:
    Make a T-shirt *77*
Jewelry *78*
Rub-offs *80*
Rubbings of Your Own Design *82*
Wall Hanging or Banner *83*
Paper Collage *85*
Iron-ons *86*
Stained Glass *87*
Greeting Cards *89*
Decorative Sketches *90*
Woven Art *91*
Other Possibilities *92*

Bibliography *93*
Index *95*

Preface

The inspiration for this book came from the enthusiasm of the many people enrolled in the rubbing workshops I conducted for the Museum of the City of New York, the Museum of Bronx History, the Center for New York City Affairs of the New School, and the America the Beautiful Fund. Groups were escorted to historic or architecturally notable locations for the purpose of "lifting rubbings" on location.

All kinds of people from varied walks of life attended these classes. I instructed people of varied ages—from five-year-olds to octogenarians. (Rubbing can be enjoyed even by people with infirmities, who can easily learn to do the work with a minimum of discomfort). My attentive class members were all able to do excellent rubbings after a single practice session. Everyone found it exciting to travel to sites and to return home with a souvenir that they, themselves, had created. The idea of going to these unique places and collecting rubbings from them met with such eagerness that my students' verve resembled that of the postman . . . "Neither snow nor rain nor heat nor gloom of night stays these couriers from the swift completion of their appointed rounds." They could not always understand my reluctance to go to an outdoor rubbing site in a rainstorm. They called the course "Instant Gratification"; especially after learning the graphite technique, which facilitated their lifting of rubbings from surfaces they hadn't imagined could be reproduced.

Rubbing is especially fascinating for people who feel they have no artistic abilities. It enables them to produce an artwork with very little skill required. When a rubbing has been completed, and you step back a few paces to admire it, there is a pleasure similar to that which the person who executed the piece you rubbed felt many years before you.

Collecting rubbings can become something of an obsession. You find it becomes necessary to rub every attractive heat register—or —oh, you don't have the design on that coal-hole cover, or, that gravestone is older than any you have. Rubbings make a unique and personal diary of a trip to anywhere. It is interesting to note that people who wish to sell rubbings to tourists find that tourists often prefer to do their own, and will purchase those done by others as a last resort.

I worked with the members of a block association who were doing a cookbook as a fund-raising enterprise to help pay for improvements on their street. They chose to illustrate the book with rubbings of architectural details from the interiors of their Victorian homes and other buildings. This made their cookbook more personal and appropriate for their project.

I taught some classes in the middle of the weekday and people sometimes requested to be excused from work for a few hours to

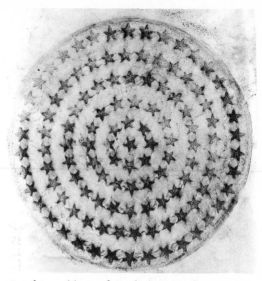

Graphite rubbing of manhole cover from historic Hunter's Point, in Queens, N.Y.

Victorian wallpaper rubbing, Central Synagogue, N.Y.C.

come to class. I found it most inspiring that on subsequent occasions they were joined in class by their employers, who had seen the results of their labors.

On a number of weekends I conducted half-day rubbing tours to a single unusual spot, like a 1920s movie palace, and found myself accompanied by a couple of hundred people—all anxious to rub! A similar crowd joined me on a trip to a cemetery on a glorious spring day. The trees were in blossom and people came in droves with baby strollers and picnic lunches—all to rub!

I took groups out to rub places in the middle of the night so as not to interfere with operations during business hours. People who watched asked how they could join such a group. Wherever we went rubbing we recruited new people who were amazed at the lovely works of art we produced so effortlessly.

The enthusiasm of all these people inspired the idea that a book that clearly explained how to do rubbings, as well as how to use these designs for craft projects, would make the opportunity to share our pleasure available to people everywhere.

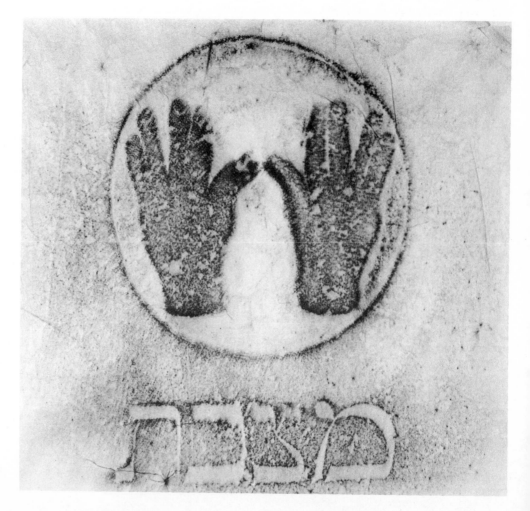

Graphite rubbing taken from Third Shearith Israel Cemetery, N.Y.C.

To those whose names follow I wish to express my indebtedness for knowledge, information, and assistance with technical problems or locating some of the sites mentioned in the text. In some instances, the rubbings that I lifted would have been unobtainable without the kind permission of others to whom I make grateful acknowledgement:

Robert Boggs, Commissioner, P.R.C.A. Administration, Bronx, New York; Albert Bruchac, Queens Chamber of Commerce; Margaret I. Carman, Flushing Historical Society; Martin Cassidy, Manager of Reproductions, American Museum of Natural History; Joan Evanish, Projects Secretary, Cathedral of St. John the Divine; Dorothy Gibb, in the office of the Rev. Canon Edward West, Cathedral of St. John the Divine, New York City; Gary D. Hermalyn, Executive Director of the Bronx County Historical Society; Barry Kugel, Executive Director, Central Synagogue, New York City; Irmgard Lukmann, Administrative Assistant, Museum of Bronx History; Loring McMillen, Director, Staten Island Historical Society; Barbara Millstein, Associate Curator, Painting, Sculpture, Sculpture Garden, Brooklyn Museum; Bert Sack, President, Civil War Memorial Committee of the West Farms Soldier Cemetery, Bronx, New York; Father Geoffrey Skriner, "St. Andrews" Church, Staten Island; Carl Stark, Mausoleum Director of Woodlawn Cemetery, Bronx, New York; Victor Tarry, Honorary Secretary, Spanish and Portuguese Synagogue, New York City; Elizabeth Tobin, Museum of American Folk Art; Museum of the City of New York; and the New York State Preservation League.

I am also indebted to the following for their help in creating projects based on my rubbings: Wendy Wesley Johnson and Patricia Bassett Chaarte of Two Needles Design Studio for their advice and manufacture of the needlepoint pillow and latch-hook rug; Marsha Sayer and Laura Zistein for their cooperative venture in doing the needlepoint stitching; Esther Barth for latch-hooking the rug; Pearl Lipton for carrying out the designs on her brass jewelry; Suzanne O'Keefe for her machine embroidery; Emily Carter for her pillowcase appliqué; Carla Grayson for her hand embroidery of the lamb; Carolyn Steinmetz for her weaving; Alexander Chowski of Century Antiques in Wilmington, Vermont, for making the stained glass; Elaine Stone, of CECE Rubbings®, for designing our greeting cards; and to Professor Eva Nambath, Assistant Chairperson of the Fashion Design Department of the Fashion Institute of Technology, for her explanation and demonstration of rub-offs.

I'm grateful to Jan Smithers and Jack Klein for letting me use the rubbings they did of English brasses; and Phil Balestrino, of Pilgrim's Progress, for the Tombstone Art® which he distributes. Thanks also to Wendy Davidson, artist in the reproduction department of the American Museum of Natural History for her fish fossil rubbing.

Appreciation goes to those people who made their collections available to me: Mr. and Mrs. Morton Lisser; Jerome S. Silverman; Dr. and Mrs. Robert Edmunds; and Matthew Marks.

I would also like to thank Ray Bentley of Oldstone Enterprises, Steve Steinberg of New York Central Art Supply, Ruth Ferman of Sam Flax, and Creative Photocopy for their cooperation.

And thanks finally to Mike Amer, Allene Talmey, Carol Fein, Kay Zentall, Jeffrey Weiss, and to my sons Conrad and Lesley, all of whom helped me in many ways to "get it all together."

Introduction

Rubbing of Mayan head from Panel of the Slaves, Palenque, Mexico.

Rubbing is a method of reproducing the surface of a carved design by rubbing or dabbing a piece of paper or cloth with various media. Generally, colored waxes, inks, or graphite are used for this purpose. It is an art that anyone can master, and it's especially nice since it's both noncompetitive and inexpensive. Since anyone can do it well, it is a particularly delightful activity for parents and children to do together. Teachers can use it as an educational tool—making rubbings can be an exciting way to learn history.

One purpose of this book is to heighten your awareness of the numberless treasures you may be overlooking on ordinary days while passing back and forth in your usual activities. Rubbing makes you more aware of the textures in your life. The coins in your pocket suddenly become something from which you can rub and arrange in a pleasing design. The sculptures in your home, the baskets, the fabrics, all become interesting, rubbable surfaces. This book will introduce you to the techniques of rubbing and direct you toward the abundance of locations for rubbing that are always nearby.

Rubbing offers the opportunity to explore the architecture, history, and peculiar art forms of any city. You can produce an original piece of art from a visit to an ancient site, like these rubbings done as souvenirs by people on visits to Bolivia and Mexico. Rubbing is also an excellent tool in landmark-preservation projects. Since much old stonework is rapidly eroding due to air pollution, or being destroyed by urban redevelopment, lifting a rubbing helps to keep a record of some beautiful objects that might otherwise be forgotten.

Decorative as well as functional objects can be rubbed. Art

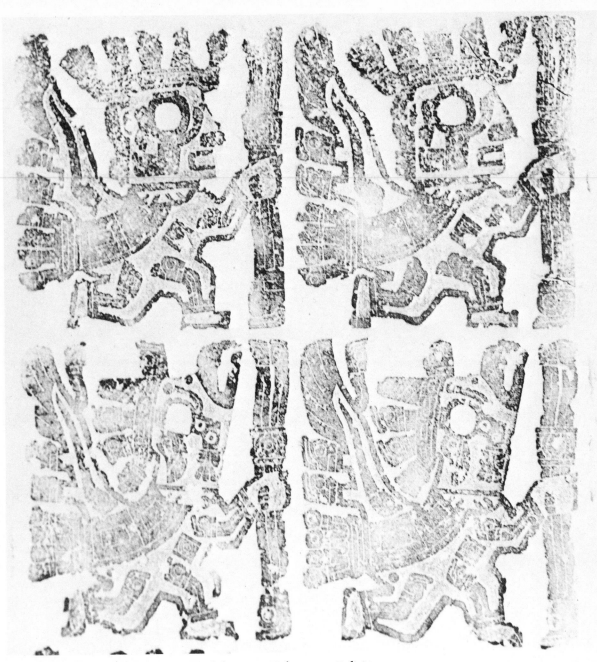

Ink rubbing from pre-Columbian monolithic gate; Tiahuanaco, Bolivia.

Deco forms cover many urban buildings and make for lovely rub-bings. Nearly all periods of art can be encountered in the larger cities, their rubbing potential only limited by one's imagination. Look down on the dated, turn-of-the-century sewer covers in the streets, or at the plaques in the pavements. Look up at the wrought-iron win-dow guards or the numerals over a doorway. Don't miss the elegant raised surfaces of some church doors. If you keep your eyes open, it's easy to find unlimited subject matter for this wide-ranging craft.

PART 1

A BRIEF HISTORY OF RUBBING

The term *rubbing* is technically used to describe the ancient Chinese technique known as *T'a-pen* or "ink squeeze." Basically, a piece of paper (generally rice paper) is placed over the surface to be reproduced. The paper is then rubbed with crayon, graphite, ink, or the like to produce a negative image. The resulting print is a rubbing.

Although the oldest known stone rubbing in existence dates from the seventh century A.D., it is believed that rubbing or "stone prints" were employed in China as early as 300 B.C. Used by the ancients as a kind of reporting or journalistic technique before the invention of the printing press, calligraphic messages were carved upon stones and placed in central areas. Travelers passing through could make rubbings of the news, returning to their communities to post the news there.

Pictorial stone carvings were also made in ancient China for the sole purpose of being reproduced by rubbing. During the Ming period, books were published from rubbings. Because it was sometimes difficult for the Orientals to visit graves, those living closer to these sites made rubbings of the gravestones to present to relatives. According to Thomas Carter in his *The Invention of Printing in China and Its Spread Westwards,* classics of the T'ang dynasty were cut in stone and people were appointed to make rubbings from them.

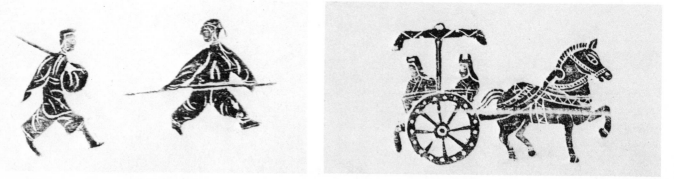

Ink rubbings of objects from Chinese Han Dynasty, 206 B.C.-220 A.D.

The Chinese method of lifting rubbings was to place moistened paper on the inscription and then to force the paper into the incised lines by means of a stiff brush. When the paper dried, a tamper of silk was touched to Sumi ink and then dabbed evenly over the surface of the paper. The paper was then removed, producing a white-on-black-background replica of the inscription.

In the mid-seventeenth century rubbings spread to Japan, where they were executed primarily in the form of *Gyotaku.* This is a wet technique, used to make impressions of fish (a way of recording the catch!). Currently, Fish Recorder Kits are available for this purpose.

In the West, rubbing has become popular comparatively recently. England is one of the most desirable places to make rubbings because the monumental brasses, done during the medieval period, are

Japanese Gyotaku rubbing.

located there. These are plaques incised with inscriptions and/or figures commemorating the deceased. The material used for them was an alloy of copper and zinc. Until the end of the sixteenth century, these brasses were produced on the Continent and exported to England. The plates are found throughout central and northwestern Europe. Currently, those in the cathedrals of England are thought to be of the highest quality. The brasses in England are most frequently found in the counties to the east like Kent and Essex.

These brasses show figures with costume, armor, heraldry, and design, and are a perfect subject for rubbing. Rubbing societies have even been organized there for the purpose of pursuing this hobby. However, lately it has become extremely difficult to obtain appointments to rub these brasses since authorities fear for their condition, and a fee is usually charged at the sites. There's hope, though, as some cities now have brass-rubbing centers that provide castings of the original brasses, from which fine rubbings can be obtained.

Rubbings are employed in many professions. Archaeologists find rubbings a valuable aid in the reproduction of carved interiors of ancient vessels. Museums sometimes use rubbing techniques when photography is not feasible, as it is sometimes possible to reproduce details by rubbing that are not clear or visible to the eye. Museums use rubbings for displaying delicate collections in an interesting and

Rubbing of monumental brass, black wax on white paper; Church of St. Mary Magdalene, Kent, England.

Rubbing—silver wax on white paper—taken from a cast of a monumental brass, done at a brass-rubbing center in London.

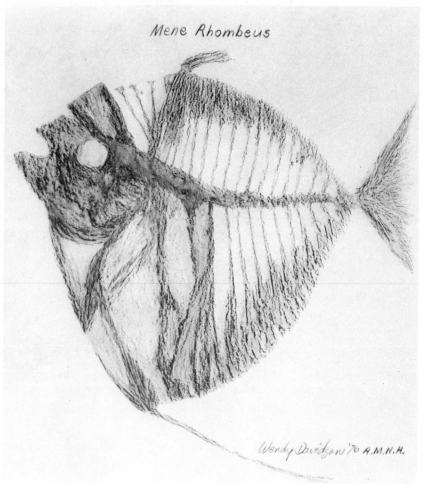

Mene Rhombeus

Wendy Davidson '70 A.M.N.H.

Fish fossil rubbing from cast, done with wax pencils on tissue paper.

attractive manner. Fossil rubbings may be done from the original fossil or from casts. A watercolor wash was applied to this wax-pencil rubbing for decorative effect. Costume designers who are interested in medieval costumery often use brass rubbings for reference. When describing clothing of this period, costume books use rubbings as illustrations—a good example is James Laver's *Costume.* The Victoria and Albert Museum also has their *Catalogue of Rubbings of Brasses and Incised Slabs,* which categorizes the brasses into costume types (legal costume, military costume, royal costume, etc.).

Historically speaking, there is one other method for "lifting" rubbings (I say "historically" because I consider it actually an abusive technique, not to be currently used), which was employed in England during the eighteenth century. The surface of the brasses to be rubbed was covered with printer's ink, after which wet paper was pressed into the lines by walking on the paper. This is similar, in principle, to the way etching plates are printed.

In the United States the graveyards of New England have until now been the most popular places from which to lift rubbings. You do not need to travel far, however. You can easily pack yourself a picnic lunch and walk to a local churchyard. If the churchyard is an old one, you'll be likely to find handsome gravestones to rub—replete with cryptograms, skull and crossbones, hearts and cherubs.

Wax rubbing from gravestone;
Brattleboro, Vt.

PART 2

LIFTING RUBBINGS: MATERIALS AND METHODS

TOWN OF MARBLEHEAD
OFFICE OF
CEMETERY COMMISSION
P. O. BOX 53
WEST SHORE DRIVE
MARBLEHEAD, MASS.

ARLAND A. DIRLAM, Chairman
HOWARD M. KNIGHT, Secretary
ROBERT L. RUSSELL

WATERSIDE CEMETERY
TELEPHONE 631-1102

BENJAMIN A. WOODFIN, Superintendent

Duplicate # 36
Fee Paid $ 1.00

GRAVESTONE RUBBING PERMIT   Date issued 8/13 19 76

Let it be known that *Cecily Firestein* an individual

residing at *NYC NY*, has permission

to rub gravestones in *Old Burial Hill* Cemetery(ies)

within the Town of Marblehead for the dates inclusive;

8/3/76 to *December 31, 76*

This permit is issued under the restrictions printed below:
It can be extended beyond the latter date upon request and may be
revoked for abusive treatment of the gravestones and or the Cemeteries'
properties, etc.

Signed *Benjamin A. Woodfin*
Benjamin A. Woodfin, Supt.

Co-signed by permitee *Cecily Barstow Firestein*

1. Use only soft brushes or a cloth to dust off the stones.

2. Use only dry materials to do the rubbings, such as astral wax or
   lumber crayon or carbon stick. Please use no inks, pastels or chalks
   or school crayons as they cannot be removed from porous stone material.

3. Stay within the limits of the paper when doing the rubbings. You are
   responsible for any damage done to the stones while making a rubbing.

4. Carry your permit whenever you go to do gravestone rubbing. Be prepared
   to show it to either the custodian of the burial ground or individuals
   of a local concerned citizen group or Police. Have proper means of
   other indentification to prove permit bearer.

5. Your cooperation in preserving our memorials, some of which are
   irreplaceable is appreciated.

TOWN OF MARBLEHEAD
OFFICE OF
CEMETERY COMMISSION
P. O. BOX 53
WEST SHORE DRIVE
MARBLEHEAD, MASS.

ARLAND A. DIRLAM, Chairman
HOWARD M. KNIGHT, Secretary
ROBERT L. RUSSELL

WATERSIDE CEMETERY
TELEPHONE 631-1102

BENJAMIN A. WOODFIN, Superintendent

GRAVESTONE RUBBINGS

PROCEDURE: A kit may be purchased at local stores. The required
materials are few and may be purchased at any art supply store: A
roll of masking tape, a large pad or roll of strong bond paper,
and a box of black lumbermarking wax crayons. Also it is REQUIRED
that you purchase a gravestone rubbing permit if you wish to do
any rubbings in Marblehead at the Cmetery office on West Shore Drive
at a fee of $1.00 per each person.

The first step is to carefully clean the stone of Lichen, dirt, and
any other foriegn matter. Next, carefully tape the paper to the
stone, making sure it sticks tightly, since the slightest shift will
cause a blurring of the design. Finally rub the broad side of the
crayon over the entire surface of the paper, being careful not to
get the wax on the stone surface. The recessed areas will appear
white while the rest will be black.

After it has been rubbed lightly it is necessary to rub again with
a firm pressure, this time working from the edges inward.

Different types of stone give different rubbings. Slate proves to
be the most satisfactory; sandstone produces a coarse texture, Schist
and Marble prove the least satisfactory.

A weak contrast in a rubbing due to the rough texture of the stone
may be corrected by touching up the black areas with a crayon. A
piece of slate can be placed under the paper to make a smooth
surface. In this way an almost imperceptible design can be made to
stand out clearly.

THE CARVINGS

Gravestone decorations represent one of the most difficult forms
of sculpture, that of low relief carving. The sculptor, confined
to a working depth of a fraction of an inch, is challenged with the
carving of forms that not only capture the spiritual quality, but also
to create the phenomenon of life like appearance. Many designers
owe part of their success to the optical illusion created by light
striking the incision at a different angle than the parent surface, thus
causing the incision to appear white compared to the darker surface.

The trade of gravestone carving at first was just a sideline job but
as time passed the demand initiated a trade. Because of the apprentice-
ship system practised at the time, the art was passed down from family
to family.

MARBLEHEAD CEMETERY COMMISSION
1972

BAW

There are two rudimentary rubbing techniques: the *dry technique,* or
wax method; and the *wet technique,* or ink dabbing. A third, often-
used method uses *graphite* (instead of wax or ink) on either wet or
dry paper.

Generally the dry technique employs a wax-based crayon or
graphite, but other pigmented materials can also be utilized. The surface selected for lifting a dry rubbing must first be brushed off carefully with a stiff brush. Next the paper is taped to the chosen surface
and the pattern beneath is roughed out with light strokes of the crayon. Then the rubbing is finished by emphasizing the design of the
carving with more heavily pressured strokes.

For the wet technique, the paper is also taped to the cleaned
surface, but more loosely than in the dry method. The paper is then
dampened with water sprayed from an atomizer, and permitted to
dry somewhat. Ink is daubed on the damp paper to bring out the design, or graphite may be used.

Two more advanced techniques are the *carbon-paper technique*
—rather complicated to master—and the *foil method,* a three-dimensional form of rubbing not generally done at the site. There's also
Gyotaku, fish rubbing, and then *Jio-ta-ku* (which we do not go into
in this book), making impressions of humans!

It is a good idea to go accompanied on your rubbing ventures,
as some of the sites are in rather isolated areas. If you are inhibited
about being a "spectacle"—and rubbing does often draw an audience
—then go with a group, and always try to obtain written permission
from authorities at the sites you want to rub.

A phone call will sometimes suffice. Be sure to get the name of
the person who has given you permission over the phone. Some
places require a small fee and a permit for rubbing. Other places,
cemeteries especially, are sometimes posted with NO RUBBING
signs. (In a cemetery in Marblehead, Massachusetts, there was a sign
that read NO RUBBING WITHOUT PERMIT. I paid one dollar for a
permit and was also presented with a procedure sheet for doing rubbings.)

Make certain that you remove any tape and debris that accu-
mulated around you during your work . . . and a thank-you note is
always appreciated by any organization that gave you permission to
lift rubbings.

The rubbings that you create will have many uses on their own,
and they can also be translated into many other forms, both artistic
and utilitarian. Needlepoint, stained glass, and latch-hooked rugs are
but a few examples. Projects are described in Part 3.

Materials

Paper

Experiment with papers. The choice is almost infinite, especially when working with the dry rubbing technique. If you're on a tight budget, you will find Kraft paper or brown wrapping paper satisfactory and attractive; even newsprint paper or paper toweling will sometimes do for small rubbings, and wallpaper lining paper and shelf lining paper are also cheap but adequate papers. Many of the papers described below are available at art-supply stores.

For the dry wax technique, when the large size of the paper is important, some people like to use tracing papers and layout and visualizing papers, which range from transparent to opaque. Most of these papers come in pads and rolls up to 42 inches in width, and in lengths of up to 50-100 yards. They are not exceptionally strong. The most fragile of these papers is architect's detail paper. Architectural sketch paper is attractive in cream colors.

Savage Widetone paper is the answer for really large rubbings. This is a seamless backdrop paper used by photographers. It comes in fifty colors, in rolls 107 inches wide and in lengths up to 50 yards. The white comes in a roll 140 inches wide by 100 feet long!

Rice paper is manufactured from the roots and leaves of the rice plant, which are soaked and cooked in large vats of water. A wire mesh frame is used to strain the suspension of macerated fibers. The frame and its fibers is put aside to dry in the form of matted sheets. Removed from the frame, the sheets of rice paper are then ready to be sold. Among the rice papers satisfactory for dry techniques are Mulberry (both regular and student grades); Masa, smooth on one side; Kochi, opaque and extra heavy; and Troya. (Although most of these papers sound as though they come from Japan, some are made here in the United States; Troya comes from Troy, New York!)

Perhaps because rubbing was first a Chinese art, using rice paper is traditional among rubbers. Personally, I do not consider it to be the best paper for the techniques described in this book. Aqaba paper, a hemp product produced in Manila, is a stronger, more versatile paper; particularly when a dampened paper is required. It does not tear as easily as other papers, and rice paper is quite fragile in comparision. Aesthetically, Aqaba is as attractive as most rice papers.

Oldstone's Aqaba paper, which I think is the best all-around paper for all kinds of rubbings, comes in rolls. It is available in white as well as in black, which looks wonderful when used with gold or silver rubbing wax. Aqaba is the best paper for the wet technique. It comes in sheets and rolls. If this paper is unavailable, Tableau paper is an acceptable substitute.

Interesting effects can be achieved by using some of the more elegant and unusual Oriental papers. Japanese Tea Chest paper comes in sheets of gold and silver and can be used interestingly with various waxes. Fantasy Paper comes in sheets 24" x 36". This paper has leaves and butterflies pressed into the layers of the paper and is most effective for rubbings. Wood veneer papers are also usable. Speedball puts out a printing paper that is satisfactory but a bit small.

Graveyard workers, people employed by cemeteries, use a paper called Blue Rubbing Paper to facilitate recordkeeping. It is actually a white paper with a purple tint, and is completely purple on the underside. This paper is taped to the stone and the surface is rubbed with a remnant of carpet. The design that emerges is light but clearly visible. This paper comes in rolls, and is available from cemetery-supply companies. It is a fragile paper, but it can be used to make a pictorial note of a subject you might later on wish to use for a permanent rubbing.

There is an almost endless variety of papers. Just look around the larger art-supply stores. One handmade paper is Nepal, the beautiful and traditional rubbing paper from the Orient. It is expensive. You can sometimes find other out-of-the-ordinary papers at reasonable prices—watch for sales and close-outs at the stores.

Some "display" papers are actually cloth or cloth-backed and are adaptable for rubbing. Tracing cloth is strong. It has a white working side with a dull finish. The back side is glazed. Sign cloth is also strong and has a smooth white surface. Ordinary cotton and silk yard goods can be used for rubbing. Tracing cloth that is half cotton and half polyester works best with the rubbing media because when you have completed the rubbing you can "set" the design by placing a damp cloth over it and then sealing it into the tracing cloth with a very warm iron. The fabrics containing synthetics hold the wax better.

Graphite paper and carbon-transfer papers are used in conjunction with rubbing papers. (Their uses are described later under *Carbon-Paper Method,* and they are employed in a number of the projects suggested in Part 3.) Carbon-transfer paper comes in a variety of colors.

A number of good English rubbing papers are available in art-supply shops in this country or by mail order from England.

Crayons and Waxes

Interesting variations of the ordinary black-on-white rubbing can be obtained by experimenting with different crayons and inks and pigments. Most exotic is gold wax on black paper. You can also employ colored tailor's chalks (available in notions stores), Cray-pas, ordinary primary crayons, lumber crayons, graphite sticks, or some of the imported English brass-rubbing supplies like Hardtmuth crayons or Astral heel balls. Lithographer's crayons or pencils can also be used. Some people have even tried shoe polish and/or lipstick.

Wax-based crayons can be used to best advantage in rubbing flat or incised surfaces. An extremely flat bas-relief can also be rubbed with waxes. The English rubbing waxes are softer and, of course, more expensive than the American gravestone rubbing wax. Rubbing

waxes come in many colors, including metallics, and are preferable to ordinary crayons because they have less tendency to smear. I use fluorescent Crayolas when I want to do a multicolored design on the site.

English heel balls, often used for monumental brasses and gravestone rubbings, are made of wax and lampblack. Shoemaker's finishing wax is a good substitute for heel ball. It comes in two types, hard and soft, and is used in shoe-repair shops as a stain for covering scratches and scuffs on leather goods. This wax cake comes in a variety of shapes and under various brand names, but is available only in a limited number of colors. White, brown, and black may be obtainable from your local shoe-repair shops.

For those who wish to make their own rubbing wax, Henry Trinick suggests the following heel-ball recipe in his book *The Craft and Design of Monumental Brasses:*

> *Russian tallow*
> *Beeswax*
> *Shellac: a natural resin, very hard*
>   *but easily melted by heat*
> *Household soap (very little)*
> *Lampblack*

The addition of shellac and lampblack in greater quantities will ensure a harder and blacker wax heel-ball. The mixing quantities are largely a matter of experience. Melt the tallow, the beeswax and a little soap slowly in a tin, then add the shellac and lampblack and keep in a liquid form over the fire. Great care must be taken not to spill or let a flame near the composition. Mix well and when thoroughly melted and mixed pour into pre-heated china egg-cups, small coffee cups or similar utensils. Something slightly larger than the conventional egg-cup is desirable. This makes an excellently shaped cake of rubbing wax suitable for large rubbings. For smaller pieces, pour the mixture into an open 2 oz. rectangular tobacco tin, and when cold cut it into strips. Never use a plastic container—the hot wax will melt it—and never cool the wax composition quickly, for the center will be the last part to cool off and as the composition shrinks a hollow or split will develop in the middle.

Large pieces of rubbing wax should be broken into smaller pieces to aid the obtaining of details in your rubbings. When on rubbing expeditions, carry your rubbing wax in your pocket or elsewhere on your person to keep it warm and ready for use, especially in cold weather.

When working on small rubbings, especially those with fine details, wax-based colored pencils are very useful. Eagle brand Prismacolors are good as are China marking pencils. Fossil rubbings are often done with these wax-based pencils. China markers wear down very rapidly: more than one pencil in a particular color would be needed for a large job.

Graphite

Graphite is a soft lustrous carbon used primarily for making so-called lead pencils and as a basis for lubrication.

Graphite is used for lifting rubbings when working on a raised surface (bas-relief). It is the easiest medium to master and can be used in place of inks or pigment mixtures.

Graphite is available in small tubes as well as by the pound from hardware stores and shops that make locks and keys. It is also available from chemical supply houses and some art-supply stores. I suggest buying it in the larger quantities. It becomes too expensive an item when bought in tiny amounts. Graphite also comes in various stick and pencil forms which you can rub with or use to emphasize already rubbed designs. It can also be purchased in paper sheets like carbon paper.

You can make a graphite mixture for your rubbings by pouring some *powdered* (not flaked) graphite into a small amount of linseed oil (any oil can be used though, even cooking oil). Linseed oil, like some others, may tend to stain your paper with a yellowish tint, but it is hardly noticeable. A colorless oil like mineral oil may, therefore, be more to your liking. Use a small plastic or tin box to mix and store this mixture. The objective is to make a paste of this combination comparable in consistency to canned shoe polish. Add the oil slowly, because it will keep thinning the mixture. Experience will help you decide how thick a mixture you prefer to work with.

Work as neatly as possible. Graphite travels far! It is washable from most surfaces with soap and water or scouring powder. When working with a graphite mixture, it is advisable to wear old clothing. The graphite comes out with washing or cleaning, but the oil residue may remain.

Ink

India inks or other waterproof inks are most often used in the wet methods. The ink is applied to the paper generally with a dauber or a tamper, using a "dabbing" rather than a rubbing stroke.

Chinese renk ink or Sumi stick ink that you grind to the desired consistency is interesting to rub with. Water-base block-printing inks can also be used, as can watercolors from tubes and water-soluble fountain pen ink. You may find it interesting to experiment with oil-base inks and pastes.

Stick, paste, powder, and paper forms of graphite.

Handy for beginners is a ready-made kit of supplies packaged as "Bokutaku" (Sumi rubbing), which can be found in some art-supply stores. It contains a round plastic box with a cake of pasty Sumi ink, a couple of dabbers, an extra supply of liquid ink, and instructions. The drawback here is the cost. It is quite expensive, having almost doubled in price recently to approximately $8.00. If you have difficulty finding it, you can write to Yasutomo and Company, 24 California Street, San Francisco, California, 94111, to find out where their kit is sold in your locale.

Bokutaku cake, ink-grinding slate, and dabbers.

Other Necessities

Aside from the materials discussed above, there are a number of other accoutrements you will find necessary when doing your rubbings. Equip yourself with a good pair of scissors, one that can be used to cut paper as well as to shear away obstructing grass and weeds. You should also have a fairly stiff brush to remove any grit or impurities from your subject. Never use a metal-bristle brush. It may scratch or damage the object you are cleaning. Masking tape or freezer tape should be used to tape your paper to the object you plan to rub. If you are working on very grainy stones, strapping tape will stick to them better. When practicing the wet technique you will need a sprayer. I use a fine-mist plant sprayer filled with water (if you're in the field, this should be carried in a plastic bag tied at the top). If you use the foil methods, rounded dowels or rounded-end sculpture tools will be necessary.

Always carry a pencil so that you can write the name of the site where your rubbing was completed. It is also wise to date it. Even when I'm not on a rubbing expedition, I carry a small notepad in my purse, so that whenever I pass a good "rubbable," I note its characteristics and location so that I can return to the site at some future date. Without notes, it is almost impossible to remember where you saw what.

When you are doing a lengthy rubbing in what is often an uncomfortable position, you will find kneepads invaluable. They are available in most hardware stores and dime stores. On very sunny days wear a hat. Carry a small packet of moist disposable towelettes for removing excess graphite from yourself.

Carrying your work and supplies around is sometimes cumbersome. A mailing tube can serve as a carrier, but a map case with a built-in handle is handier and sturdier. A hole can be punched into each end of a mailing cylinder, however, and a cord attached so that you can sling the tube over your shoulder. It is simple to carry your paper, rolled up, in such a tube—both before and after your rubbing is complete. I prefer to carry all my supplies, mailing tube as well, in a large, waterproof canvas bag. The bag I use is a machine-washable coal carrier. The only thing I don't put in the bag is rubbing wax, which, as mentioned before, should be carried on your person to keep it warm enough for use.

Methods

Dry Method

Of the techniques for making rubbings, the easiest is the dry technique. A dry rubbing is accomplished by simply covering the surface to be rubbed with a piece of paper and rubbing the paper with a crayon. One should experiment a little at home first. Choose some raised items (for example, coins, leaves, doilies, etc.) and cover them with

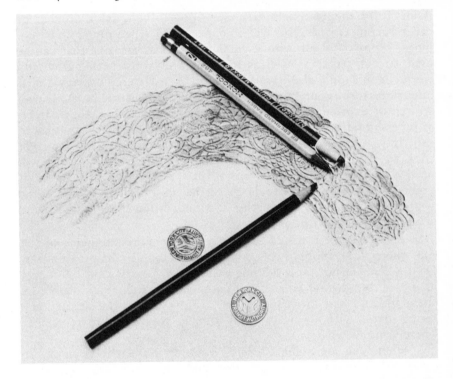

ordinary paper. Pencil over them with a soft pencil or crayon. Right away you will probably see a few of the practical problems. It is necessary, for example, to have a suitable object to rub. The pencil may tear the paper. The crayon marking may overlap the design. The paper may move around, etc. All these annoyances are easily overcome with practice. Once you're comfortable working with familiar objects, you'll be ready to go out and search for new ones in the field.

For your first field trip, either choose a rubbing site that interests you particularly, or one that is convenient to your home. Go equipped with the correct materials. If you go to a place where you feel it would be better to have permission, get it! Once there, look

for an object with a clear, incised design. Choose a subject that is in relatively good condition, not one with a severely eroded surface. In old graveyards, for instance, brownstones are usually in better shape and easier to work from than are markers of sandstone or other materials.

For the dry technique, you will need the following:

1. Opaque but tough-quality good paper, preferably a rice or hemp paper in large sheets or rolls; heavy-weight tracing paper is good too, and Kraft paper will also do (it's inexpensive and especially good for youngsters, as is wallpaper lining paper)
2. Masking tape or freezer tape
3. Kneepad
4. Fairly stiff brush (never metallic bristles)
5. Scissors for cutting paper or for cutting away grass or weeds
6. Rubbing media (gravestone rubbing wax, heel ball, graphite, carpenter's crayon, etc.)
7. Large cylindrical tube for carrying paper and supplies
8. Piece of nylon stocking
9. Small flat piece of cardboard

Before beginning your rubbing, brush the subject free of any impurities. Do this *gently* so as not to damage the object (never use a wire brush). It is not necessary to do a thorough job here. If you're rubbing a gravestone, you might also wish to clip any long grass that might interfere with your work. You are now ready to begin.

Settle down on your kneepads and tape your paper, preferably with masking tape, securely and smoothly to the object you want to rub. Use strapping tape over the masking tape on very grainy surfaces. Cover the object well, so that your rubbing medium will not slip and mar it. This is an appropriate time to mention that when you are rubbing small, free-standing items it is preferable to tape the object to the paper as though wrapping a package. This arrangement will minimize the chances of either the object or the paper moving away from the other.

Inexperienced rubbers may find it an aid to feel the design with their fingers as in Braille, before rubbing with wax. To begin the rubbing, lightly go over the entire surface with the wax to expose the raised portions. Next, broadly darken and begin to block out the complete design with the flat side of your crayon or wax. This is done by holding a small flat piece of cardboard at the edge (feel with your fingers) of the design so that out-of-bounds crayon strokes hit the cardboard instead of the paper. Following this blocking-in procedure, you'll see the design more clearly, and be able to decide where you want the rubbing to appear darker or lighter. Complete the rubbing by repeating the process where necessary with a heavier pressure. It is possible to peek at the design underneath if you are uncertain as to its breadth by loosening the tape at the bottom, making sure the rest of the taping is secure, and looking under the paper. Replace the loosened tape and continue working. Never lift off the whole paper to see the surface underneath as it will be virtually im-

Before going outside, try out the dry technique on an object at home. In this case, a brass fireplace accessory is used.

Tape paper smoothly and securely.

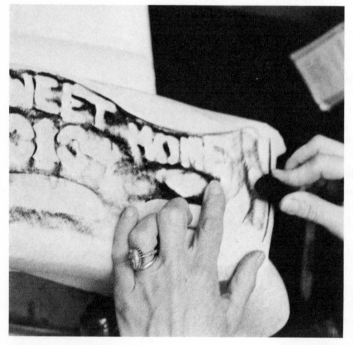

Go over entire surface with wax.

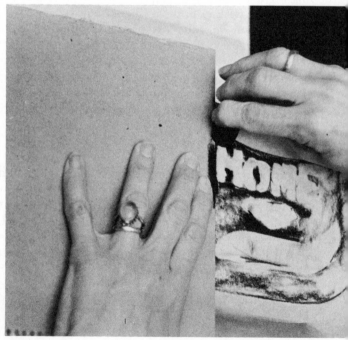

Block out the rubbing with cardboard and flat side of wax.

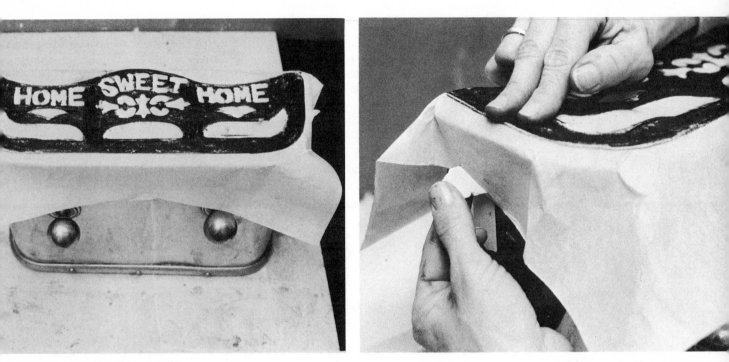

When you're satisfied with the finished product . . .   *peel tape off, away from the paper toward yourself.*

possible to reposition it exactly. When you are pleased with the result, the rubbing is finished. Some people like to go over the completed rubbing with a nylon stocking to give it a sheen. Gently peel the tape away from the paper toward yourself.

The process you have completed is termed, by the cognoscenti, "lifting a rubbing." Most smears or unwanted lines can be erased with lighter fluid or cleaning fluid or a rag soaked in paraffin.

It's possible to obtain a rubbing with a positive (as opposed to the usual negative) impression, although this method requires a good deal of patience and care. You'll find it simplest to use a white or light-colored wax crayon and proceed to do the rubbing as described above. After completing the rubbing, use India ink to carefully blacken in the unwaxed spaces on the waxed side. Allow the ink to dry completely. Saturate a clean cloth with cleaning fluid and wipe off the areas covered with wax. Only the dark lines of the ink will remain and you will have a positive print. Carry out this process in a well-ventilated area, away from flame, and preferably not at the rubbing site. You can also use dark wood stain in place of India ink over the wax rubbing. The stain will be "resisted" by the wax, and will give the rubbing an antiqued look. To improve the appearance of the finished product, cut around the rubbing and mount it on mat board.

A variation on the dry technique is to replace the wax with a graphite-in-linseed-oil emulsion—a paste, actually. (Directions for making this emulsion can be found on page 24.) The same papers may be used—I prefer hemp paper. The resultant look with the graphite is more like a sketch, and has a dark gray, rather than black,

29

color when finished. Although wax media work best for rubbing an incised surface, graphite will be more successful when the surface is somewhat raised. These two methods can also be combined. I prefer to use the wax first and then go over it with the graphite. If the detail of your subject is unclear, it sometimes helps to go over a wax rubbing with graphite while the paper is still taped to the object. This often helps to emphasize what is underneath.

To use a graphite paste, dip a soft cloth wrapped around your index finger into it and then wipe most of the graphite from this cloth onto another piece of cloth. The idea is to remove all impurities and clumps of graphite from your wrapped working finger. Ex-

Art Deco panel from elevator door in the lobby of the Waldorf-Astoria Hotel in Manhattan (graphite with oil).

Rubbing of gravestone of World War I hero combines wax methods on smooth portions, graphite on rougher stone.

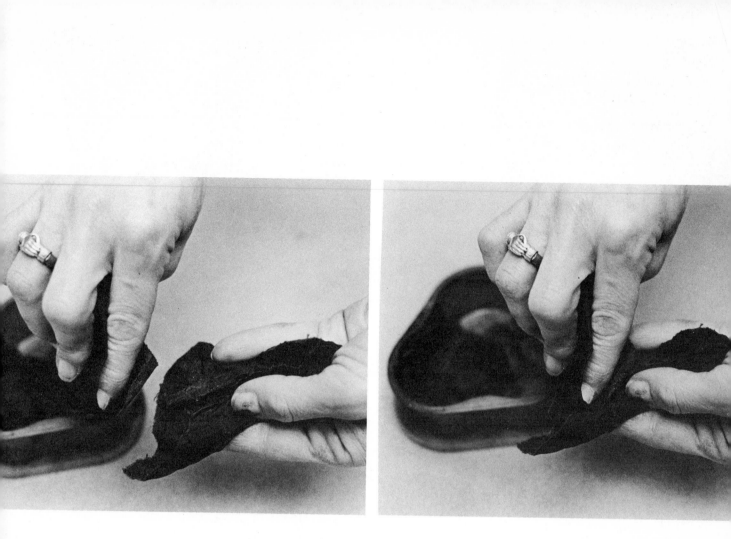

cesses of graphite cause smearing and dark spots. "Less is more." You can always darken an area afterward. The initial rubbing should be light. Feel the design with one hand and spread the graphite with the other until you have "rubbed" the entire design. For larger surfaces you may prefer to use cloth wrapped around several fingers: the work goes faster this way. You can make the design more like a drawing by going over, with more graphite, those places where you think shadows would emphasize its three-dimensionality. Some people call this method "dabbing," as they prefer to make a "dabber" of chamois to work with, rather than using a soft rag. I believe this is unnecessary and prefer to "feel" the surface underneath, using my fingers as the dabbers. Of course, you could use the chamois itself in place of cloth. If you find that you still pick up too much graphite on your cloth and your work looks smeary or too dark, wipe the rag's excess graphite onto paper toweling or newspaper before applying it to your paper.

Since working with graphite is somewhat messy, take along something to clean your hands off with (little pre-soaked wrapped towelettes are good as a temporary measure). Soap, water, and a nail brush gets it off your hands quite satisfactorily.

The paste's oil holds the graphite in place, so I have not found it necessary to use a fixative to prevent the finished rubbing from smearing. If you wish, however, you can further ensure the preservation of your work by coating it with a spray fixative.

Use a stiff brush to clean around a coal-hole cover.

Tape paper so it lies flat.

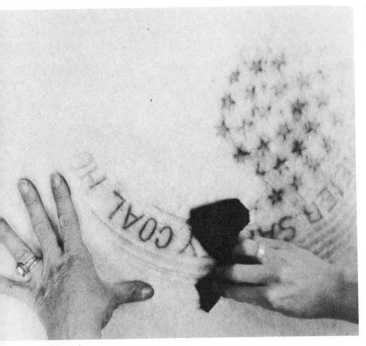

Feel design with one hand, apply graphite with the other.

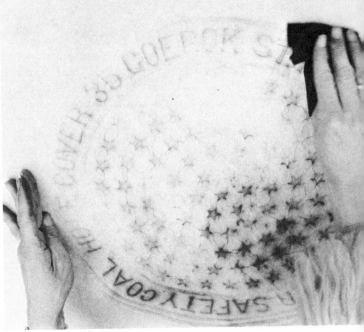

Continue rubbing, darkening where desired.

Rubbing is finished, ready to be untaped and rolled up.

Wet Method

As your enthusiasm is fired by the idea of all the interesting sites you have yet to visit for the purpose of lifting rubbings, you might want to add the "wet technique" to your repertoire. It is also a "dabbing" process, and is most suited to uneven or deeply carved surfaces and medium-high bas-relief. This method for obtaining architectural details from buildings might, however, be frustrating for beginners since it is difficult to control.

A "wet" rubbing, broadly speaking, is made by attaching the paper to the object, dampening the paper, and tamping the paper-covered object with ink so as to produce a negative image on the

Wet rubbing taken from doors of the Cathedral of St. John the Divine, N.Y.C.

paper. The resultant image appears softer and grayer (rather than blacker) than one produced by dry rubbing, but darker than one produced with graphite.

You'll need the following supplies for the wet technique.

1. Rice or hemp paper
2. Masking tape or freezer tape
3. Kneepad
4. Fairly stiff brush
5. Scissors for cutting paper or for cutting away grass or weeds
6. Fine-spray bottle or mister
7. Plastic bag for carrying sprayer and water
8. Container of water
9. Dabbing media (Sumi ink or water-base ink) and dabbers (one about 1½ inches in diameter, the other a bit larger)
10. Soapless hand cleaner or moist disposable towelettes

Practice and patience is required to perfect the techniques of the wet method. You must be careful not to wet the paper too much —or too little. You must also try to get a uniform amount of ink on the dabbers each time, and to remove any impurities that may collect on them.

First, gently clean the object and tape your paper to it, though somewhat more loosely than with the dry method. Use your sprayer to dampen the paper. Start about two feet away and coat the paper with a fine water mist. Do not soak the paper, just moisten it. Give the paper about eight minutes to dry somewhat, depending on the

To get the feel of the wet technique, start with something at home.

Wrap object loosely with paper.

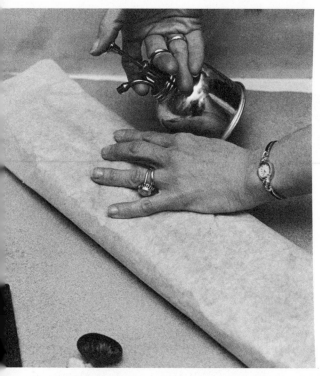

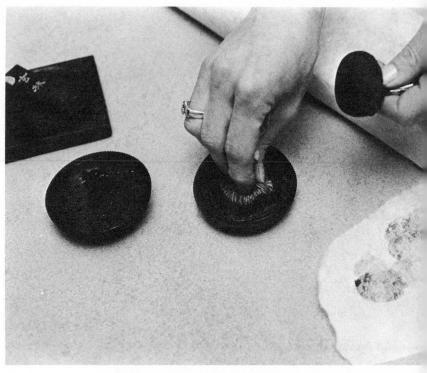

Moisten (don't soak) paper with a fine mist, then mold to shape of object.

When paper is nearly dry, dip smaller dabber into ink.

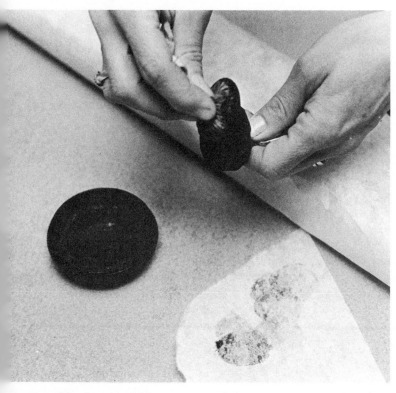

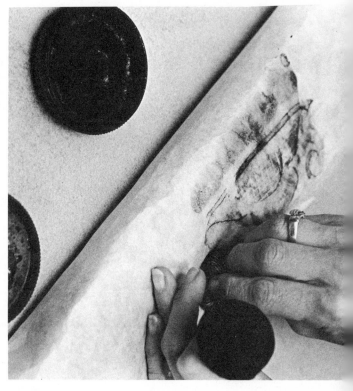

Transfer ink to big dabber. Try out ink consistency on scrap paper.

Dab paper, remoistening where and when necessary.

humidity and weather. If necessary, retape the paper to smooth out any wrinkles and/or air bubbles. Remember, the paper should be fairly loosely taped. Now, gently but firmly mold the paper with your fingertips to the object's surface; loosen tape and paper further if still too taut. Just before the paper is completely dry, apply the ink by taking the smaller dabber and dipping it into the water-based ink or the ink paste. If you are using Sumi ink and the paste seems a little dry, add a bit of liquid ink (comes with kit) or spray ink cake

Finished product has a soft, dark look.

with water. Give it time to be absorbed. Then, transfer the ink to the larger dabber by rubbing it with the smaller dabber—this gets rid of any grainy impurities. Dab the surface of the paper with the dabber. Do not rub or stroke. If the paper should appear dry in certain spots, remoisten it with a paper towel or spray it lightly: the ink will not run. If you find that too much ink has collected on the dabbers, tamp them on newspaper or paper towels. Continue with the dabbing procedure until your project is completed. As mentioned before, practice is required to get the "feel" of this technique. Experience will tell you how much ink to apply and how wet the paper should be.

When finished, remove the tape and paper carefully. You can roll up the paper and put it in the cylinder when dry, though it's preferable to place the paper between two large sheets of blank newsprint for flattening and drying. You can weigh down the papers for reinforced flattening. The rubbing can also be rolled up when damp, and weighted down and flattened at home.

Incidentally, in all techniques mentioned here, papers may be ironed on the back sides with a cool steam iron. It is necessary, however, to protect the cover of your ironing board.

If you wish to make your own "wet kit" and save some money, line the bottom of a covered plastic box with a sponge cut to fit snugly. Soak the sponge with Sumi ink. (This ink comes already prepared, or you can grind Sumi ink stick in a special slate saucer.) Don't flood the sponge, just moisten it well. Make two dabbers with two small sponges, by scrunching each of them up and putting each into a circular piece of soft fabric and binding this with a rubber band. Pure silk is the preferred fabric. As mentioned on page 25, ready-made Sumi kits are available in many art shops, or through their distributor, Yasutomo and Company, in San Francisco.

You can also use acrylic paints, block-printing inks, and dry pigments instead of Sumi ink for this method. When working with certain hemp paper, however, the stickiness of some paints may pick up the paper fiber and tear the paper.

A more complicated wet technique, to be used with inks that contain little or no water, is described by John Bodor in his book, *Rubbing and Textures.* Rather than taping your paper to the stone, he suggests moistening it with a combination of methyl cellulose and water, which will simultaneously cause the paper to adhere to the stone and dampen it. Then, after the paper dries and before ink is used, he recommends brushing the surface of the paper with beeswax, which prevents the ink from penetrating the paper. At this point one proceeds, as above, with the ink-dabbing process.

My own preference in wet methods is one which employs an oil-and-powdered-graphite paste, the same mixture described on page 24. The difference here is that before applying the graphite, you spray a hemp paper with water until it is quite damp. You can, at this wetness, see the design under the paper to some degree. Loosely tape the paper, and, as you apply the graphite paste, sort of mold the paper to the surface you are rubbing. This technique is especially good for somewhat higher reliefs, and I find it easier to control than the ink version of the wet method. You are less likely to get results too dark or smeary in certain areas. This technique also looks most "artistic" to me—rubbings made this way are soft, resembling charcoal sketches.

An iron gate is a good candidate for the oil-and-graphite wet technique.

Tape paper loosely.

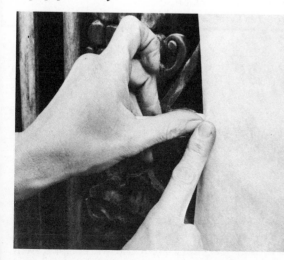

Spray hemp paper until quite damp; retape if necessary.

After dipping a cloth into the paste, begin to rub, molding paper with other hand.   *Completed rubbing will have a "charcoal" effect.*

Carbon-Paper Method

If you are really into rubbing at this point and are concerned that you are missing a technique, you may wish to experiment with yet another, the carbon-paper technique. When exploiting this method, you'll need a gentle touch, or you will be frustrated by torn paper and a large, wet mess. The color of the carbon paper determines the color of the rubbing.

The materials you need include the following:

1. Fine rice paper (for example, Deberasu)
2. Masking tape or freezer tape
3. Kneepads
4. Fairly stiff brush
5. Scissors for cutting paper or for cutting away grass or weeds
6. Plastic bag
7. Spray bottle
8. Water
9. Carbon paper or graphite paper (comes in large sheets); use artists' variety, not typewriter carbon
10. Plastic burnisher
11. Spray fixative
12. Newsprint paper

Clean the stone and attach your paper directly to it with masking tape. As in the wet technique, lightly spray the paper with water. Since we are using a very fine rice paper here, the water spray will cause the paper to become limp. It is necessary now to loosen the tape and gently restretch and retape the paper. The paper will contract as it dries. Add additional tape to keep paper firmly in place.

When the paper is *thoroughly* dry, take a large sheet of blank newsprint and tape it to the top rear surface of the stone, folding it over so that it hangs downward over the front surface and covers the rice paper. Next, take a sheet of graphite or carbon paper and place it carbon-side-down, toward the stone, but *between* the newsprint and the rice paper. Keep the carbon paper in position with one hand and rub over the newsprint with plastic burnisher. Gentleness is in order. When completed, it is advisable to spray the rubbing with fixative to prevent smudging. (You'll find the carbon paper's impression to be a lovely piece in its own right.)

A casting from the uppermost part of a tombstone is used for this carbon-paper rubbing.

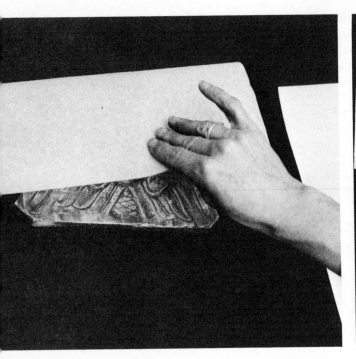

Tape rice or hemp paper to object.

Spray lightly; retape (or, in this case, wrap and retape) paper around object. Wait until dry.

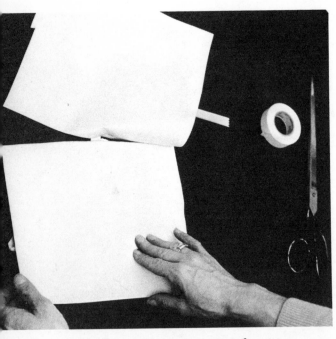

Then tape blank newsprint to top rear surface; insert carbon paper between the two other papers, carbon side down.

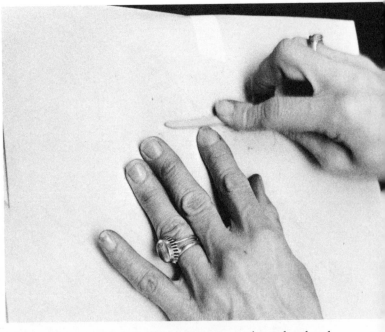

Fold newsprint over carbon; hold in position with one hand and burnish with the other.

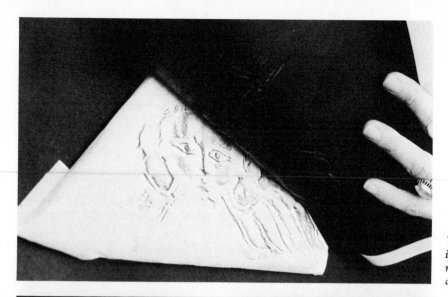

You can glimpse the development of the rubbing if you lift up only one section of the carbon-and-newsprint, keeping the other section firmly anchored.

Finished carbon rubbing.

A handsome by-product: the carbon paper itself, complete with imprint.

The wet and dry methods are the classic rubbing techniques, the dry method being the paradigm. There are a few other modes which deserve mention: the foil technique, which is a three-dimensional form of rubbing; and *gyotaku*, a Japanese fish-printing technique.

   The foil method, in particular, may be enthusiastically utilized by those with a special interest in crafts.

The raised design on this coal scuttle lid is well suited to the foil technique.

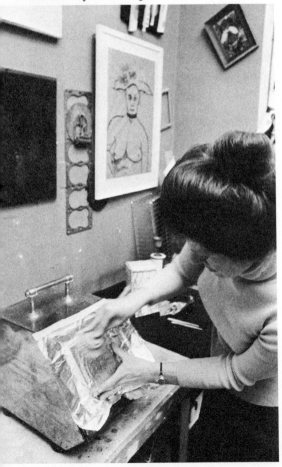

Foil Method

The foil method is really a form of metal tooling or plaque making. Practically speaking, it is not convenient to complete the process at the site.

The basic supplies required for the foil technique are:

1. Heavy-duty kitchen aluminum foil
2. Assorted plastic burnishers
3. Casting plaster (plaster of paris)
4. Container for mixing plaster (plastic bowl or large coffee can)
5. Container of water
6. Masking tape
7. Fairly stiff brush
8. Flat file or sandpaper
9. Kneepads, if necessary

We begin this technique, as all the others, by cleaning the surface to be rubbed. Cut a piece of foil twice the length you need to overlap the design you wish to reproduce by a few inches on all sides. Fold the foil in half to create a double thickness. Tape the folded foil to the surface with masking tape. Rub your fingers over the foil, making rough contours of the design underneath. Once you are aware of the placement of the design, use a brush or burnisher to rub it onto the foil. It is best to work out from the center of the design so as to push aside the excess amounts of foil. Continue this process until your design looks sharp and has good relief. Remove the tape; then lift the foil from the design. Carefully fold all edges of the foil so as to make a shallow pan. This is to be the mold, so use masking tape to reinforce all corners, and to seal any holes that may have been caused by too much rubbing pressure on the foil. In the mixing container, combine plaster of paris and water to a smooth consistency. (Three parts plaster sifted into two parts water seems to work well. Use your hands to mix!) Pour this mixture into the foil mold (making certain the side of the design you wish to show is on the outside surface of the foil). If you want to hang the finished mold, insert a picture-hanging wire into the plaster after about ten minutes—after fifteen minutes, the plaster will have started setting, and it will be too late. Permit the plaster to harden and dry completely for at least ten hours.

When the plaster has hardened, carefully lift the mold from the foil. Smooth all rough edges with a file or sandpaper. You can now paint or decorate the mold according to your taste.

Tape foil, contour roughly with hands, then brush.

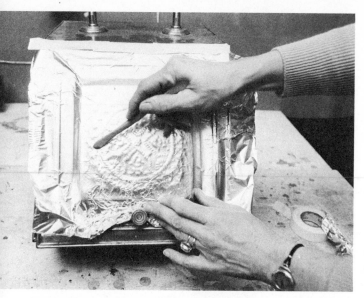

Working from center, burnish to bring out greater detail.

Remove foil, bend up edges to make a shallow pan, and pour in plaster.

When hardened, lift mold from foil.

Darken mold with graphite or paint if desired.

Gyotaku

Gyotaku (pronounced gio-ta-ku) is the Japanese art of "fish rubbing." It is basically in the wet-technique category, and uses tampers or dabbers to convey the ink or watercolor to the paper. Sometimes ink is applied to the fish itself, which is then covered with sturdy Japanese paper. Next, the back of the paper is rubbed with the fingers, and then the paper is removed to obtain a print of the fish. You might want to experiment with this method at home or try it on your next fishing expedition.

Reproducing Your Rubbing

Rubbings reproduce very well. They can be used to make greeting cards, bookmarks, and posters. A unique way of reproducing them is to use the negatives (rather than the positives), obtained by photostating your rubbings.

Rubbings may also be reproduced for illustrating newsletters and bulletins. Central Synagogue, for instance, a national landmark in New York, illustrated its handbook "A Walking Tour of Central Synagogue" with rubbings rather than photographs.

Greeting card, using negative photocopy of wet-technique rubbing on page 33.

Storage and Display of Rubbings

It is, at this point, practical to discuss both the mounting and storage of your rubbings, as you may accumulate quite a large collection.

If you wish to display your rubbings, there are several ways to do so. The most conventional is to frame them, as you would any print or watercolor, with frame, mat, and glass. Considering how large many rubbings are, this method, although attractive, can be quite expensive. Once you pass the standard-size mat board, everything becomes inflated in price. You then need special, larger sheets of glass, and the frame, of necessity, must be thicker to accommodate the heavier weight it has to support. Glare-free glass also adds to the cost. However, if you have only one rubbing to frame, or several smaller ones that you want in matched frames to coordinate with your decor, this may be a very satisfactory solution.

Plastic box frames are light and attractive, and rubbings look good in them. Art-supply stores often discount something from the price, but these frames, too, become relatively expensive as they increase in size.

A process called "museum mount" or "shrink wrapping" is an excellent way to display and preserve your rubbings. Basically, the rubbing is mounted on a foam board, and then together they are covered with a clear plastic wrap that is heat-sealed on the back side of the board. It is a process not unsimilar to the way food is wrapped and sealed in the supermarket. A hanger is attached to the back. The lightness of the end product is an advantage, as well as its air-tight seal. Very attractive, it is a bit less expensive than glass and frame. Some commercial packaging firms will do an inexpensive shrink-wrap job for you if you have a quantity to be assembled. The one prerequisite for the cheaper price is that all the work be of equal size.

Another attractive, and less expensive, mounting can be done by "dry mount," a process by which a print is bonded to cardboard by using a special, heat-sensitive adhesive tissue. Framers sometimes do dry mounting, but specialists in photo mounting are more likely to have the proper equipment. It is impractical to dry mount your rubbings yourself, since the necessary presses are rather expensive. Rubbings can also be dry mounted onto cloth.

Positionable dry-mounting adhesive is a new product that makes it possible for you to mount your work yourself to resemble a dry mount. This adhesive transfers to the back of the rubbing to be mounted. You place your rubbing face-up on the adhesive sheet and then lift it up. The adhesive transfers to the back of the rubbing. It is then prepared to adhere to a board. It forms a permanent bond when burnished down into its final position. (Burnishers for this purpose are available where the adhesive is sold.) Adhesive sheets are available up to 16" x 20". The so-called permanent bond can be safely removed with rubber-cement solvent. The manufacturer claims this product will not dry out, discolor, or stain (3M Positionable Mounting Adhesive no. 567).

You can, of course, also mount your rubbings on sheets of museum-quality rag mat board with white glue.

An English firm puts out an inexpensive hanger which is exported to the United States. It's made of two strips of grooved plastic, and you slip top and bottom of the rubbing into these strips. The top piece has a string attached for hanging. Rubbings may be varnished for an antique appearance.

Those rubbings that you don't frame can be rolled up and stored. Mailing tubes or wine-bottle cartons keep rolled-up rubbings in place. If at some future time you wish to display them, you can flatten them by ironing them on the wrong side with a warm iron (making sure to protect your ironing board) and/or by laying them out flat and pressing them by covering them with heavy books or other weights. When you do roll up rubbings, it is a good idea to secure them with a rubber band and slip a piece of paper under the rubber band with an explanation of what is rolled up. Rubbings may also be stored flat. Remember, always label them with date, place, and any other pertinent facts.

Sources of Supplies

Retailers

The following "big city" art-supply stores routinely carry the rubbing supplies you will need for all the techniques mentioned in this book. If none of these stores is close by, just look under Art Supplies in your classified directory. It is always wise to call the store first to make sure that the supplies you require are in stock.

East Coast

Arthur Brown & Bros., Inc.
2 West 46th Street
New York, NY 10026
212-265-7100

This store has a good stock of inexpensive papers to experiment with and map cases to hold supplies in.

Sam Flax (main store)
55 East 55th Street
New York, NY 10022
212-481-4700

Sam Flax has a few conveniently located stores in the city. Small student discounts are given.

New York Central Art Supply Compamy
62 Third Avenue
New York, NY 10003
212-473-7705

This company caters to "rubbers." A catalogue of rubbing supplies is available. They carry many English products, and specialize in handmade papers. Steven Steinberg will be most helpful.

Graphite rubbing taken from plaque in Sculpture Garden, Brooklyn Museum, N.Y.C.

Pearl Paint Co., Inc.
308 Canal Street
New York, NY 10013
212-431-7932

Relatively reasonable prices.

Kostos Framers
3251 M Street, N.W.
Washington, DC 20007
202-333-4277

Midwest

Chagrin Art Supply
Chagrin Falls, OH 44022
216-247-3287

Labidie Arts, Inc.
240 W. Michigan Avenue
Kalamazoo, MI 49006
616-342-2472

West Coast

Baby and Company
5404 Seward Park Ave. South
Seattle, WA 98118
206-622-4077

Craft and Folk Art Museum
5814 Wilshire Boulevard
Los Angeles, CA 90036
213-937-5544

Creative Merchandizers
785 Andersen Drive
San Rafael, CA 94901
415-453-7346

Rubbings
214½ Main Street
Neveda City, CA 95959
916-265-6111

Mail-Order Suppliers

If you don't mind waiting, mail-order suppliers can often provide superior products and more helpful service than an overly busy art-supply store:

Graphite rubbing, Vermont gravestone.

Cecily Firestein
Box 5070
F.D.R. Post Office
New York, NY 10022

Oldstone Enterprises
77 Summer Street
Boston, MA 02110
617-542-4112

This firm specializes in stone-rubbing supplies, and sells wholesale to stores as well as retail to individuals. They put out a complete "Gravestone Rubbing Kit," packed in a large cylinder. The company also has manufactured for them, in the Philippines, a hemp paper called Aqaba. It is strong and supple and not too expensive. There is a postage-and-handling charge on retail orders.

The Pilgrim's Progress, Inc.
Box 31B, RD 1
Honesdale, PA 18431

Both wholesale and retail, this company distributes Tombstone Art®, i.e., casts of designs taken from gravestones, and sells rubbing kits and materials.

Phillips and Page
50 Kensington Church Street
London, W8, Eng.
01-937-5839

This English firm is a good mail-order supplier for dry-technique supplies and books on the subject of rubbing. Catalogue available.

Graphite

Occasionally it is a problem to find graphite. If so, write to the company below, and they will send you a list of distributors in your area.

Dixon Crucible
Graphite and Lubricants Division
167 Wayne Street
Jersey City, NJ 07303
201-333-3000

Mr. George Black has been a most helpful resource here.

Paper

"Blue Rubbing Paper," no.504R, may be ordered from this company. The paper measures 25" x 100'.

King and Malcom Abrasives
57-10 Grand Avenue
Maspeth, Queens, NY 11378
212-EV 6-4900

Shrink-Wrap Packaging

Package It, Inc. (quantity)
767 Third Avenue
Brooklyn, NY 11232
212-768-7375

Ask for Mr. Jerry Greenberg, proprietor.

Mark LV Frames Ltd. (single items)
386 West Broadway
New York, NY 10012
212-226-7720

PART 3

PROJECTS

Now that you have a collection of rubbings, graphic mementos of places visited and objects enjoyed, you can consider translating some of your favorite designs into crafts projects. Rubbings, you'll find, lend themselves to a variety of terrific-looking, useful articles—embroidery, jewelry, needlepoint, posters, hooked rugs, T-shirts.

To get you started, this section will offer a variety of plans and ideas to transfer those prized rubbings into other creations. Lest enthusiasm be dampened by lack of skill, you'll find that the projects described are fairly elementary. More advanced variations and procedures are suggested in books listed in the bibliography, should you be inspired to engage in more refined projects. And remember, any local crafts shop will usually be able to offer additional advice and suggestions.

Art Deco graphite rubbing from perfume factory, Long Island City, N.Y.

Linocuts

Rubbing designs transferred onto linoleum blocks and carved out, either in relief or cut-away, can make wonderful hand-blocked prints for fabrics and papers. Such block printing is inexpensive and works on a quite uncomplicated principle: the material or paper is simply stamped repeatedly with an inked block carving.

For the project below, I used an Art Deco design taken from a perfume factory. Since I had only one rubbing of the motif and did not want to ruin it by penciling it in order to transfer it, I did what should be done with any irreplaceable design—I traced it.

Tracing is simple and effective, if you keep a few things in mind. First, secure the original to a table with masking tape, and then, just as securely, tape a piece of architectural detail paper over it. You are now ready to trace the design. Use a pencil, aided by a triangle to keep the lines straight.

After completing the tracing, tape a piece of carbon paper, face down, onto a linoleum block. (Mounted linoleum blocks are available in art stores; and are really more convenient than ones you might try to put together on your own.) On top of the carbon, place the tracing, also face down, and go over the lines, pressing heavily with a pencil. The design on the tracing paper is put face down so that when the completed linoleum block is printed, the design will not be a mirror image. The architectural detail paper is, of course, transparent enough to show the lines on the reverse side. After you have finished tracing the design, remove the papers. You might wish to darken the lines on the block with your pencil or a permanent marker.

Design transferred onto linoleum block.

You are now ready to begin cutting the linoleum block. By means of gouges, you'll either cut away the design, leaving the background in relief, or *vice versa,* gouging out the background and leaving the design in relief.

The cutting tools required for your first linoleum cut can be purchased in an inexpensive kit, consisting of a handle with about six cutters of various sizes and shapes which screw into it. (These kits are available in art-supply stores and Japanese arts-and-novelties shops.) As you become more adept at linocuts, you may want to invest in more professional tools and gouges.

You will also need a brayer, or ink roller (one six inches wide and made of plastic, rubber, or tough gelatin will do the job), and a few tubes of oil-base block-printing or fabric inks. These supplies are all available in art and crafts stores. The oil-base inks are considered permanent. In addition, you'll want a slab of glass or plastic on which to roll out the inks. A piece of battleship linoleum, purchased in a floor-covering shop, or an extra linoleum block to practice on before you proceed would also be good to have around.

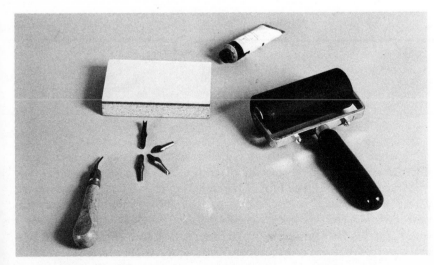

For our purposes, the most straightforward direction to take is to start gouging out the background. Care must be taken not to dig too deeply into the linoleum. If the cutting tool becomes imbedded, it will cause the topmost surface of the linoleum to fragment instead of forming a definite line. It is always important to keep your fingers behind the tool so that if it slips you are not stabbed with it. Keep rotating the block as you try to cut curves. Hold the tool firmly, pushing it with your right hand (if you're right-handed) and turning the block with your left hand when necessary.

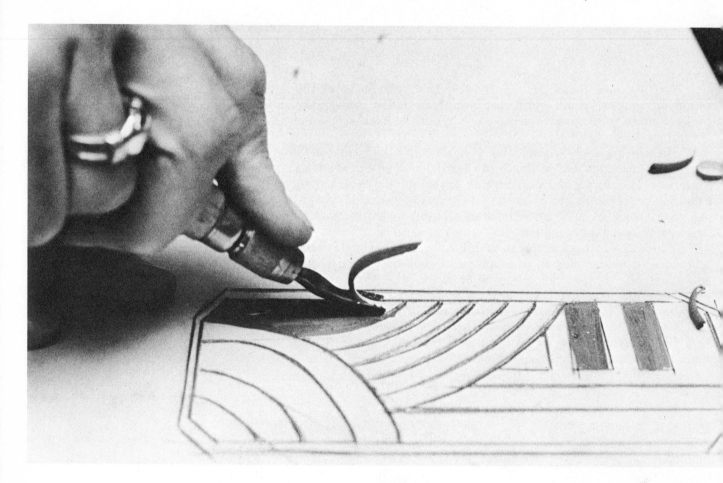

When the design has been cut to your satisfaction, squeeze some ink out on the slab of glass or plastic. Use the brayer to spread the ink, and then to ink the block. When inking the block, roll the brayer across it repeatedly to cover it with an even film of ink. Use the thinnest possible coat of ink that will provide the color density you require. In this first linoleum project, we'll do a one-color print, as separate procedures are required for prints of more than one color.

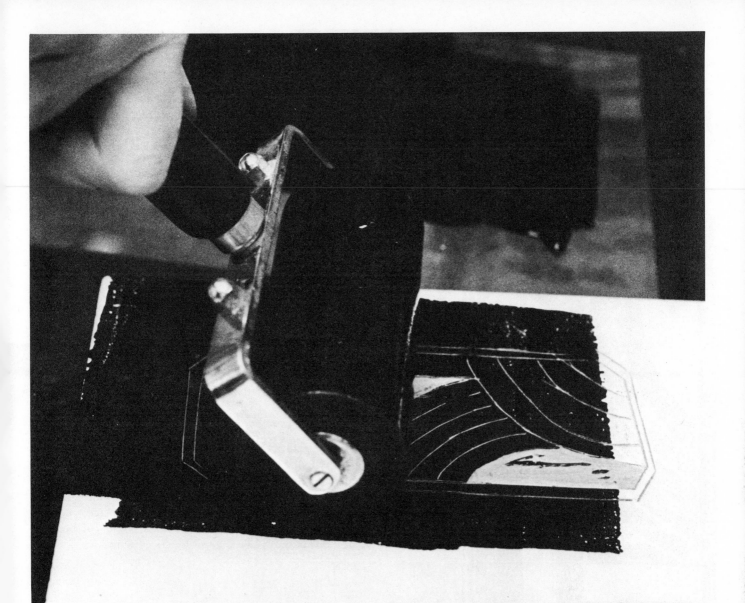

Printing can be done by burnishing. Place the paper or fabric on top of the block's inked surface and rub the back of the material with any smooth, rounded item like the back of a tablespoon, a burnisher, or a rice paddle. Take care to keep the paper or fabric from wandering around the block.

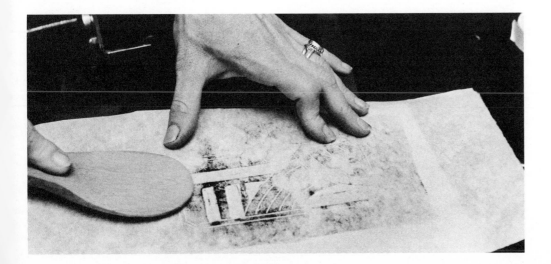

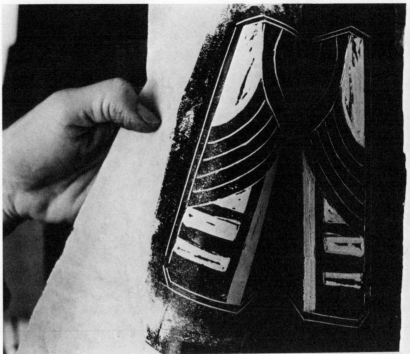

If you'd like to elaborate on the finished lino-print, try hand-painting over it when dry with fabric paints or acrylic paints. This would be particularly effective on clothing, especially denim.

The process for making woodblocks is similar to that for linocuts. Simply transfer your rubbing to a woodblock surface, and proceed from there. The following section provides some further suggestions for using your rubbings to make objects of wood.

Woodworking

Transfers from rubbings to wood can be used as free-standing, three-dimensional designs secured to a base, or as cutouts painted and hung from strings, like mobiles, or as wall decorations. The designs can be traced and then burned into wood with a wood-burning pen. These burned designs can be used to decorate coasters or the tops of home-made wooden boxes.

Painted Cutouts

The aim of this project is to translate a rubbing design into a decorative wall plaque.

I traced a stylized angel from a gravestone rubbing onto a piece of plywood. The original rubbing was taped to a table with masking tape, and then covered with a large piece of architectural detail paper (which comes in rolls). I then traced the portion to be cut out of the

Graphite rubbing from Trinity Churchyard, Wall Street, N.Y.C.

Rubbing design transferred onto tracing paper.

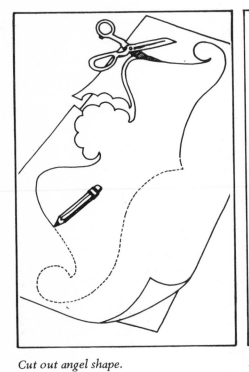

Cut out angel shape.

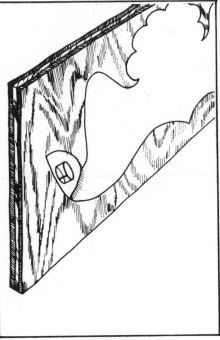

Retape shape from underneath to wood.

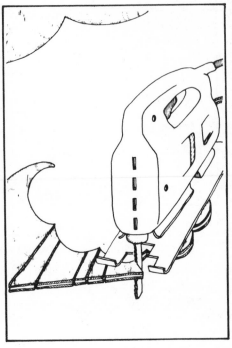

Cut wood, following pattern.

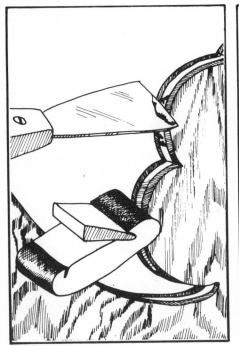

Fill in any gaps with wood putty. Sand.

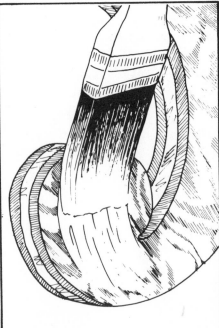

Paint surfaces with gesso.

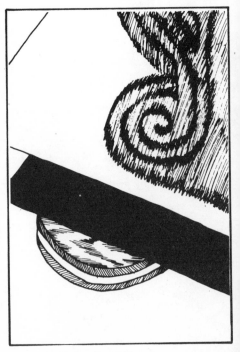

Trace angel details with carbon paper onto piece.

Paint in details.

wood, removed the tracing paper, and cut out the angel shape, and then retaped it to the piece of plywood. The plywood was next cut with an electric saw along the edges of the paper pattern. The edges of the cutout were then filed and sanded to make them smooth.

The wooden angel was to be a painted interpretation of the original rubbing. The wood was covered with two coats of gesso and then the angel was traced on top of that with a large sheet of carbon paper (graphite paper, which comes in large sheets, may also be used). Gesso is a brilliant white ground for painting upon. It gives a brilliance to the paint colors applied to it. It also provides a smooth surface to work on, and seals the wood. The rest of the figure was painted with acrylic waterproof paints.

Finished product.

Electric woodburning pen.

Woodburning

This project was used to make an angel headboard for a bed. A rubbing of an angel was used as the central portion of the design.

The second angel shape was easier to cut out than the first, for all I needed to do was to place the first plywood angel on a board, trace around it with a pencil, and then proceed to cut it out with the electric saw. As before, I traced the rubbing, using a large sheet of graphite paper, onto the cutout angel form. Then I filed and sanded the edges.

For scorching the surface of the wood I used a woodburning kit purchased from a toy store. However, I would not suggest that you purchase such a kit just for such a project, since it doubles the cost of the pen by supplying you with various worthless items. You will need an electric pen and some screw-on overpoints. These points enable you to get varied effects with the pen and permit you to reduce the amount of heat when desired. Colored foil can be applied to the finished woodburning through the use of an overpoint.

To start your woodburning project, plug your pen into an electric outlet and permit it to heat up for several minutes. (Be certain that the pen has a U.L.—Underwriters' Laboratory—rating, which attests to the safety of the pen's wiring.) The tip becomes very hot, so do not touch it to test the temperature. Have a piece of scrap wood for testing temperatures and practicing strokes. Always lay your pen on its side, on a fireproof surface, when not in use.

Follow the outlines of the tracing with the point or sharp edge. With practice, you will find that by angling the pen you can achieve variations in the depth and width of the lines. Move the point only as fast as it burns the wood. Regulate depth by pressing harder and moving slower. After you have completed outlining your plaque it is

Angel cutout with woodburning designs.

possible to shade it with the pen or tint it with paints. To achieve a solid, dark background, place the flat surface of the tip in contact with the wood and move slowly until you get the color you want. For textured effects you can cross-hatch or burn dots into the surface.

I used acrylic paints in the brown family to shade my woodburning, although other kinds of paint or even wood stains can be used. Colored foils or gold leaf may be applied to your plaque. This is done by placing the shiny surface of the foil in touch with the pen and the dull side in contact with the wood. All materials should be held in place with tape. Use an overpoint to reduce the temperature of the pen and then proceed to trace your pattern right over the foil. Burn through the foil. The point must stay in contact with the foil as interrupting contact causes a break in the line. Foil decoration of your plaque cannot be erased: it is permanent, so work precisely.

Varnish or shellac your plaque when completed. Mount it for your purposes whether it be a top for a box, a headboard for a bed, or a base for a lamp. You may prefer simply to attach screw eyes and wire and hang your creation from the wall. Wooden pieces could also be added or strung to this piece to make a mobile from your plaque.

Your woodburning pen may be used to burn designs into cork or leather. Use overpoints, since a cooler point is required on these materials. Rubbing border designs would make a lovely pattern for a belt, or coasters could be made by burning floor-tile details into cork.

Your woodburning pen may also be utilized as a wax-sculpture tool, for candle sculpting.

Wood Carving

You can use your woodburning as a tracing for a wood carving. Here I will discuss only incised carving, as it is a relatively simple type of carving. Other phases of carving are dealt with in books specifically on the subject.

As in the wood painting and burning, the first procedure is to transfer your design to the wood. Then, using a carving knife, a cut about 1/6" deep is made on the line. Then angle the knife about 15° and make another cut just outside the line toward the outside of the design. This process will remove a thin sliver or shaving of the wood. Always cut in the direction of the grain. You may embellish your design at this point by stippling the background or by continuing to remove the back grain with your knife or by leaving some sections in high relief and others in low relief.

Stippling can be done by repeatedly hitting a thick nail with a hammer until you cover the surface you wish to texture.

After your carving has been completed, dust your work and sand if necessary. Wood may be stained. The stippling, for example, may be stained dark and the raised areas left in the natural wood color and shellacked.

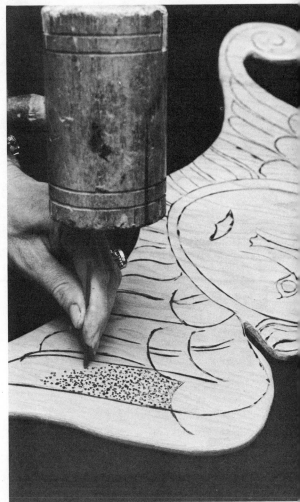

Stippling.

Appliqué

Many of the simpler designs, those done primarily from wax rubbings, can be adapted to appliqué. I suggest wax designs for this purpose, rather than graphite ones, because the former generally are not shaded.

I selected a Victorian gravestone to use for a hand-appliqué motif on a pillowcase, and made the rubbing in duplicate. One of these

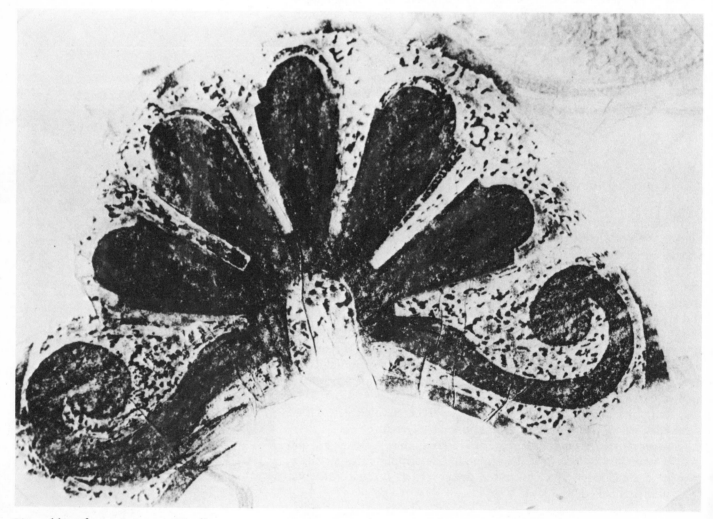

Wax rubbing from gravestone: Woodlawn Cemetery, Bronx, N.Y.

served as the actual pattern. It was cut apart into several components of the design, and then each of the paper elements was laid upon a piece of fabric and pinned to it. Next, each form was traced onto the fabric, allowing about ¼" beyond the border of the design to turn

under for hemming, and then cut out. (Hemming the cutouts gives each piece in the appliqué a more finished appearance.) The paper pattern may be discarded now. The pillowcase fabric itself was chosen from one of those used in the appliqué in order to provide a cohesive overall design. Each segment of fabric was pinned to the pillowcase and then stitched onto it, following the arrangement of the duplicate rubbing that was left intact. As each piece was sewn on, the straight pin was removed. After completing the appliqué design, a ruffle was sewn to the edge of the pillowcase. The completed pillowcase was then ironed.

A motif similar to the one above could be carried out on the top edge of a bed sheet as well as on bathroom towels. This would create a unique coordinated bath-bedroom ensemble. You can, of course, make up a similar project using a sewing machine rather than hand stitching.

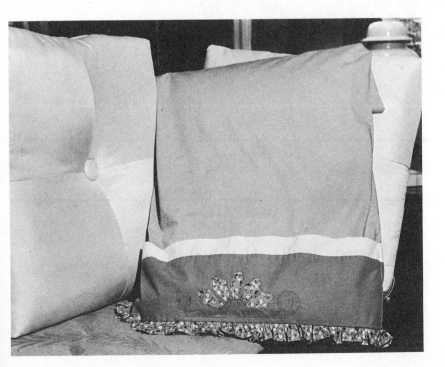

Hand Embroidery

This section deals with a relatively elementary style of hand embroidery or "free embroidery." Advanced, or elaborate, embroidery stitches may be learned from embroidery handbooks. This embroidery was done by a young child, and shows how rubbing projects can be adapted to a youngster's talents as well as to the talents of those with advanced embroidery skills.

Wax rubbing from brass medallion; transept, Cathedral of St. John the Divine, N.Y.C.

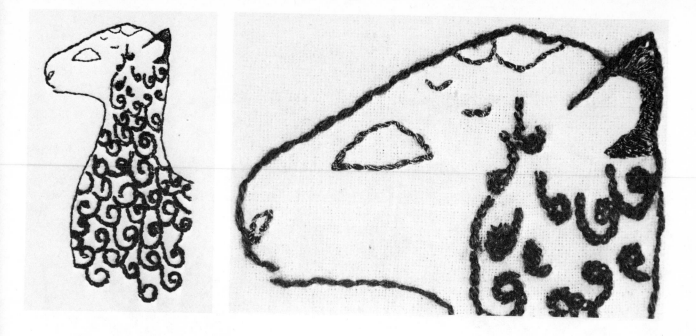

For purposes of hand embroidery, there are three different methods for transferring your rubbing design, depending on the opacity of the fabric you will be working on. If the fabric is quite transparent, you can trace your design directly onto the material with a soft pencil. If, however, the fabric is thick or textured, you will need to first trace the design onto tracing paper or dressmaker's pattern paper and paste the paper into position on your embroidery fabric. It will then be necessary to go over all the lines of the rubbing design with small running stitches. Carefully tear the pattern paper away before you begin the embroidery. The sketching stitches are removed once the embroidery is completed. The third method utilizes dressmaker's carbon. The carbon paper is positioned face down on your material and the design over that, and you then go over all the lines of the design with a pencil or a tracing wheel (this may damage the rubbing). This procedure is described in more detail in the section on wall hangings.

The kind of embroidery threads to use depends upon the type of embroidery you wish to create, but all must be colorfast. Use embroidery or chenille-type needles and a thimble. An embroidery hoop helps to maintain evenness and keeps the work flat—making it easier for you to stitch. The hoop is placed over the section you are working on by first stretching the fabric gently and evenly across the smaller hoop and then pressing the slightly larger one over it. This keeps the fabric taut and helps prevent puckering of the stitches. You will also need scissors for snipping threads.

The prominent groups of stitches used in free embroidery are flat, knotted, crossed, looped, and linked. There are also composite types as well as filling stitches and couching stitches. For specific instructions for these and other stitches, I recommend *One Hundred Embroidery Stitches,* a booklet put out by Coats & Clark Company. The booklet costs about fifty cents.

This embroidery of a lamb, based on a rubbing taken from the Cathedral of St. John the Divine, was worked primarily with a chain stitch and satin stitches.

Your completed embroidery project can be used as part of an upholstery, made into a pillow, or simply framed.

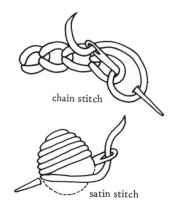

chain stitch

satin stitch

Victorian design done with colored crayons;
Woodlawn Cemetery.

Machine Embroidery

Machine embroidery can be a most creative and unique experience. It provides textures that cannot be duplicated by hand. The addition of colored and metallic threads and/or appliqué provides the sewer with all kinds of original possibilities. Zig-zag machines increase the varieties of stitches you can manufacture, but straight-stitch machines can supply you with enough techniques for a most satisfactory project. Machine stitches are varied by tension adjustments, and machine embroidery usually requires a tension somewhat looser than for normal sewing. Be sure to read your machine's instruction manual before loosening or tightening the upper tension. An embroidery hoop may be used with a sewing machine.

Transfer your rubbing design to the fabric you wish to embroider with transfer paper or by using dressmaker's carbon. Carbon or transfer papers are best used on washable fabrics, and ensure maximum accuracy of reproduction. Trace your design with a pencil onto

tracing paper. Then pin it, face down, to the base of the fabric and press over it several times with a hot iron. When you remove the tissue the imprint on the tracing paper will appear on the fabric. Make allowances for reverse images if you are using lettering.

This design was done mostly with a stitch called satin filling. It requires practice and familiarity with machine sewing. It is important to have the correct feed on the machine for this stitch; if you sew too rapidly, the machine will jam. Begin by loosening the top tension to zero. (Leave the bobbin tension unchanged.) Remove the presser foot on the sewing machine. Keep fabric taut by using a hoop. Move the fabric within the embroidery hoop, from side to side, and a bit forward with each line, until you fill in your design with horizontal lines.

The stemlike shapes in this machine embroidery were done with a trapunto stitch. This was accomplished by putting another layer of fabric under the design area and sewing straight stitches along the stem design. The presser foot was kept on the machine. Several rows of straight stitches were used on either side of the stem for emphasis. A tunnel was created under the stem in this way, and venetian-blind cord was threaded through it to achieve the finished trapunto effect.

Doll or Pillow

What fun to make a doll from one of your rubbings! An easy way to begin is to purchase a simple doll pattern from one of the commercial dress-pattern companies. I chose one from Butterick ("Huggable Polly Pal"). I cut out and used their basic pattern, but traced my angel head in place of theirs and drew the facial features accordingly (you could, if you prefer, paint them with acrylics). I also made a pattern of the angel's wings and added them to the back of the doll. When making a fabric doll use muslin, jersey, brushed nylon, or felt in any flesh color. Follow the pattern.

Stitch the front and back pieces together leaving an opening so that you can turn the doll inside out. Start stuffing with one pound of polyester fiberfill or small cut pieces of old nylon stockings. Stuff the arms and legs first. Use a rounded, wooden spoon handle to pack tightly. Stitch across arms and legs. Stuff head and remainder of body in the same way—close opening. Make hair out of yarn and attach. Your doll can be decorated with sequins, beads, feathers, or additional embroidery.

A pillow could be made from the same doll pattern by eliminating the body and using only the upper section.

Graphite rubbing from bas-relief; outside walls, American Museum of Natural History, N.Y.C.

Trace pattern onto canvas.

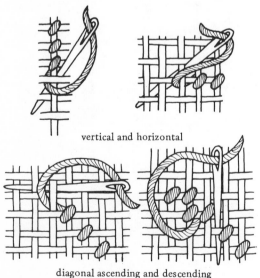

vertical and horizontal

diagonal ascending and descending

Needlepoint stitches.

Needlepoint

It is possible to trace your own rubbing design onto a needlepoint canvas. However, if you decide to do it yourself, there are certain limitations you should be aware of. For a start, it is easier if you do not choose tightly curved or highly detailed patterns. It should also be kept in mind that a needlepoint is not a photographic reproduction —it is more like an interpretation.

The rubbing of this ram's head, a bas-relief from the stone walls around New York City's American Museum of Natural History, was reduced by the photostatic process. Take your rubbing to a commercial "stat house" or photocopier and ask them for a "positive photostat" in the size you require. Next, go to a needlepoint store and purchase mesh of the appropriate size. The size is determined by the amount of detail in your pattern. A 14-gauge canvas was used for this ram's head needlepoint. The next step is to darken the lines of the photostat with a marking pen. Place the canvas mesh over this and use push pins to hold it in place. You will be able to see your design quite clearly through the canvas. Use oil or acrylic paints or an indelible pen to paint your design on the canvas in the colors you want for your finished needlepoint (see latch-hooked rug for illustration of this step). Before stitching let your painted representation dry thoroughly. Acrylics dry faster than oils. Then use Mystic tape to reinforce the raw edges of the canvas to prevent the canvas threads from unravelling. (If you feel unsure of your ability to transfer the stat of the design yourself, take it to a needlepoint studio, where a professional will handpaint your design on the canvas.)

The next step is to purchase the yarn. If you are new to the craft, you can ask at your needlepoint shop how much and what type of yarn your design will require. This ram's head was stitched with two-ply Paterna Persian yarn and will be, when finished, a pillow.

Thread your needle, knot the yarn, and begin stitching. Stitch from right to left diagonally or from top to bottom vertically. Use different stitches in various areas—changing stitches causes less stress in one direction on the canvas. (If you know only one or two types of stitch, use the stitches pictured here or consult a needlepoint book to learn a greater variety.) When you come to the end of your yarn, weave it into the back of the canvas. When you have finished stitching, it may be necessary to block your needlepoint. Blocking is a service provided professionally by some shops or you can follow these step-by-step instructions for blocking, provided by 2 Needles Limited Editions, Inc.:

Blocking

1. When you have completed working your design your canvas may appear diamond shaped because stitching has a tendency to distort

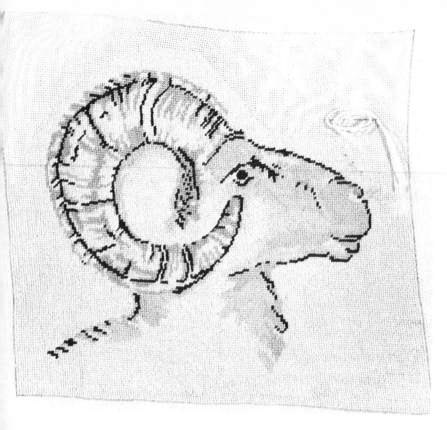

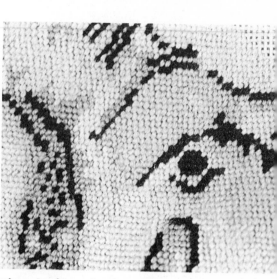

Close-up of ram's head in needlepoint.

the original shape. To block your own canvas proceed as follows.

2. Cover a board (½-inch plywood is perfect) with paper toweling or muslin and onto it draw the outline of your canvas according to the original dimensions you recorded before beginning to stitch.

3. Dampen the entire back surface of your canvas with cold water until the water just begins to soak through. (If canvas has become soiled in handling, immersing it in a mild solution of Woolite is advisable.)

4. Lay the canvas face-side down onto the covered board, line up an edge with the outline and tack down two corners. Stretch the canvas so that the other two corners match to the points on the outline. Tack them down. Since most tacks, push pins, etc. tend to rust upon contact with wet canvas and/or wool be cautious and stay as far away as possible from the stitched edge of the design.

5. With the corners aligned and fastened, start on one side and with a generous supply of tacks or pins tack down the edges at half inch intervals always matching the edges to the outline. As you come to the third and fourth sides you may have to tug a bit on the damp canvas to bring it to the outline but it is quite safe to do so . . . your canvas will not tear. Let it dry for 48 hours or so.

6. When the canvas has dried thoroughly remove it. It should have returned to its original shape indicating that the blocking has been successful. Should your canvas require another blocking, however, the second time is easier and should be all that is necessary. After blocking your canvas is ready for finishing.

A needlepoint can be made into a variety of items like a tennis-racquet cover, a wall hanging, a cover for an appointment book, a lingerie case, or a decorative mounting for the front of a pocketbook or a pillow.

Graphite rubbing from supporting columns, Central Synagogue, N.Y.C.

Latch Hooking

A latch-hooked rug can be made by using latch-hook canvas. Transferring the design is done in the same way as for needlepoint. When making a rug you will probably need to enlarge your original design. All other procedures are the same, except for the actual latch-hooking process. Starting at the center of the canvas simplifies the work. Use washable yarns. If your design is very large, you may need to whipstitch additional pieces of canvas together.

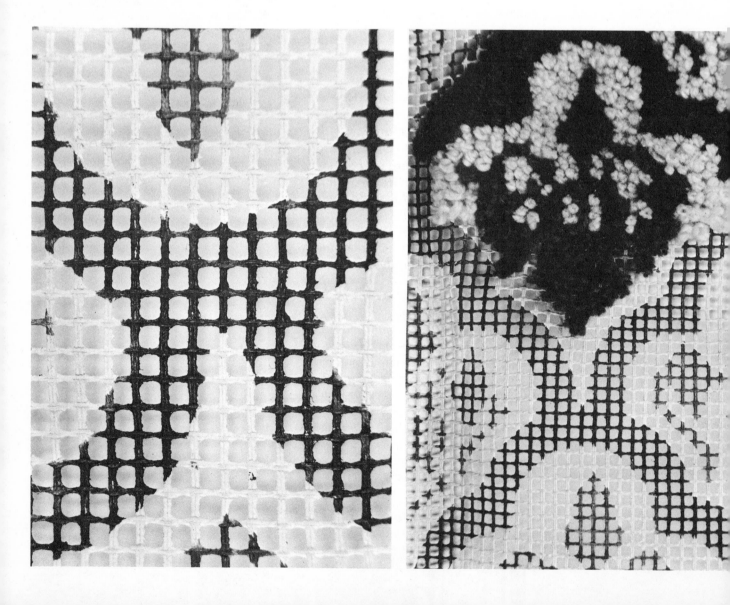

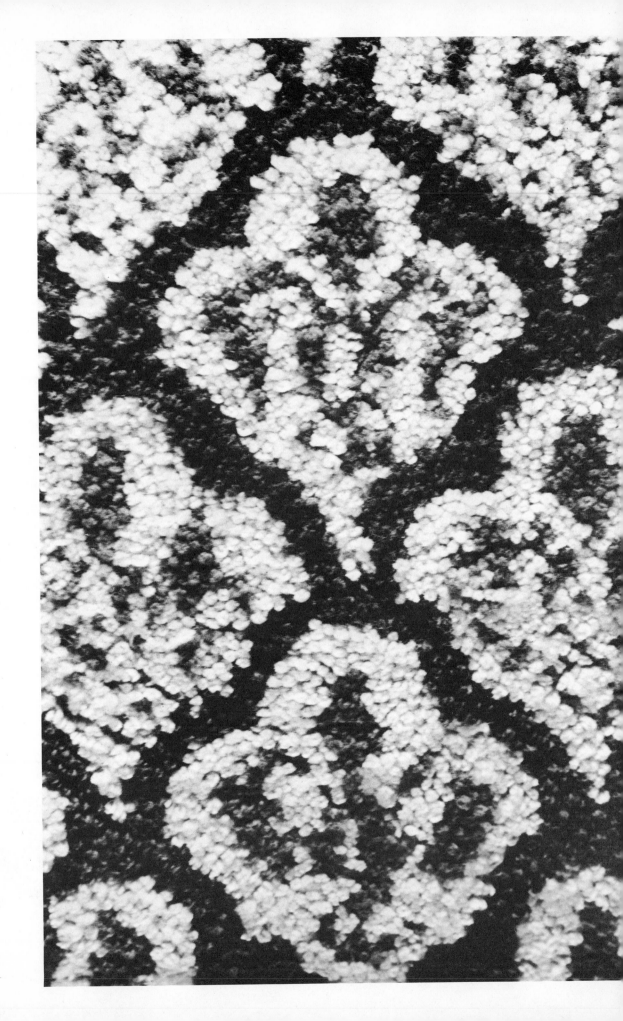

Stencils

Stencils can be made from rubbing motifs and then traced and repeated. These stencils may be used to make designs on skirts, sheets, napkins, ties, or tablecloths. To take the stencil idea a step farther, rubbings can be translated into silkscreens and then used for printing.

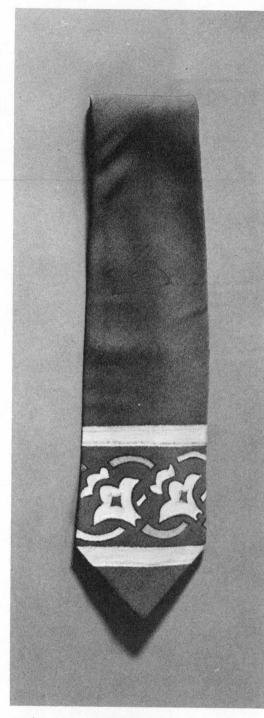

Necktie, onto which stencil design has been outlined and then hand-painted.

Wax rubbing from floor tile.

Stencil cut out from rubbing tracing.

and Silkscreens

Silkscreening is a printmaking technique used to produce multiples of a design. In general, a silk (or other mesh) cloth is stretched over a wooden frame, and a design is affixed to this cloth screen via a stencil. The printing consists of forcing colored ink (with the help of a squeegee) through the screen in those areas not blocked out by the solid sections of the stencil. An advantage to silkscreen prints is that screen stencils do not print a mirror image, as is true in other printing methods. The motif on the stencil and the printed design will both face in the same direction. Any type of bond paper may be used for the stencil as long as it is absorbent, transparent, and lies flat. Stencil paper, available in art-supply stores, is preferable, however. The necessary screens can be purchased complete from art-supply stores as well.

To illustrate using a rubbing as the design idea for a serigraph (a silkscreen print), the most rudimentary silkscreen process will be used: that involving a paper stencil. Begin by placing your original drawing on the printing base and marking off register lines. These lines enable you to properly place each sheet that is to be printed. Cut three small pieces of cardboard and glue these in place with rubber cement next to the register lines—these pieces serve as registry guides.

The next step is to place tracing, stencil, or bond paper over the original. Center it and tape it in place. Using an X-acto knife, trace the design onto the stencil. Try not to cut into the original drawing underneath it. Do not take the elements apart at this point but do mark those pieces you do not want to print. This will point out the pieces you will need to remove when you are ready to do the "stripping," i.e., clearing to prepare desired areas to receive the ink. Lower the screen. Spoon or pour some stencil ink across the part of the screen near the hinges. Draw the squeegee (a strip of soft rubber set in a handle) across the surface of the silkscreen. When you open the screen you will see that the entire stencil has adhered to the underside of the silk. Leave all pieces there that you want to use (a little rubber cement may be used to hold the small pieces if necessary—apply rubber cement through the silk on top). Leave all pieces there that you want to print. "Strip" the others.

Remove the original drawing from the base. Insert a piece of paper in the register lines to print on. Lower the screen and squeegee ink across the surface of the silk. Raise the screen and remove the print. Repeat this process until you have the desired number of prints. Prints may be hung with clips from an indoor clothesline to dry.

When you have completed your silkscreen project, lift off the stencil, discard it, and wash your screen with a cleaner appropriate to the type of ink or paint you have used.

Wax rubbing from floor tile, the basis for napkin design.

Tracing, from which stencil is made.

Squeegee spreading ink across silkscreen.

Silkscreen design printed on luncheon napkins.

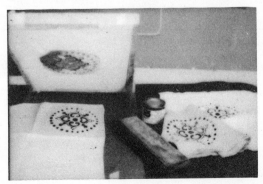

To make stencil: Take original rubbing, mark register lines, and glue down cardboard pieces as guides.

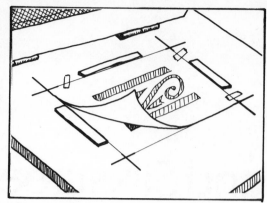

Place stencil paper over original and tape in place.

Trace design onto stencil with X-acto knife. Mark areas to be stripped.

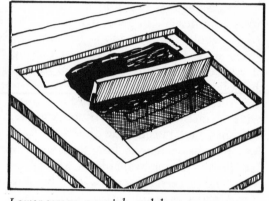

Lower screen, pour ink, and draw squeegee across surface.

Lift screen; stencil will adhere to silk. Strip the pieces you've marked from the stencil, which will be ready for printing.

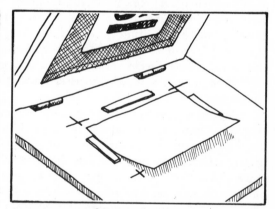

Insert paper or fabric within register lines.

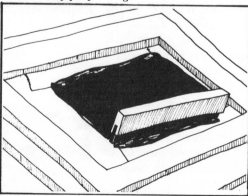

Lower screen; ink thoroughly.

Raise screen; print will be ready to be removed.

Photographic Color Transfers: Make a T-Shirt

Wax rubbing of sewer cover; Bronx, N.Y.

Another process used for printing or transferring rubbing designs onto fabric is a photographic or technigraphic process done with a computerized copy machine. This is not a technique you do yourself; instead, go to a copy center and the machine operator will reproduce your rubbing on a fabric surface for you. Basically, what the machine does is to produce a matrix, or master copy, of your rubbing on specially treated paper. This reproduction is in the form of an "iron-on" transfer. Multiples can also be made this way. The machine can reproduce pictures on many types of paper and fabric; however, certain fabrics need to be specially treated before printing can proceed. (Your design can be printed onto artist's canvas so that you could do an oil painting of your rubbing.) Some of the machines can even reproduce images onto metal, wood, glass, or other surfaces.

Some of the limitations to keep in mind when utilizing the photographic transfer process (sometimes called the "color-in-color transfer system"): The image to be copied, currently, can be no larger than 8½" x 11", and the reproduction is a mirror image of the original, i.e., the copy is made by placing the original material face down on the "object glass" of the copy mechanism. Therefore, it will be necessary to have a film positive made of any lettering you wish to use in your design. This will add to the cost of reproduction.

One copy center I visited utilized a 3M color machine. The machine is quite astonishing in that it can reproduce the image you feed it identically or it can be programmed to alter the copy from the original. The system, "3M Color-Color System II," changes the color of your printed rubbing to any one of a myriad variety of colors you choose. This particular mechanism can also enlarge or reduce the proportions of your image. The instrument makes a copy in about thirty seconds. The machine can also be programmed to delete colors, and to adjust for color density.

If, for example, you are having a T-shirt printed, be sure to specify, in writing, exactly what is to be done with your garment and what color printing you want, etc.; otherwise you may be displeased with the result. Do not forget to tell them what size shirt you require if they supply it. The finished product is supposed to be washable in cold water and mild detergent.

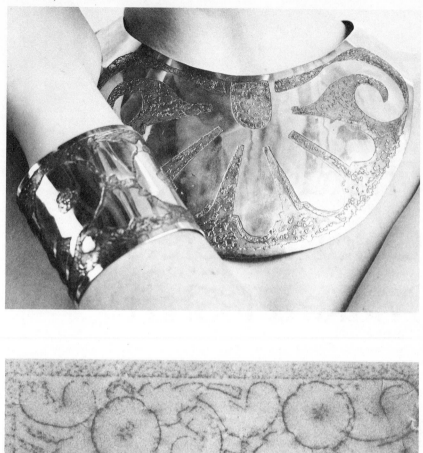

Wax rubbing from detail of tombstone (for necklace).

Graphite rubbing from detail of tombstone (for bracelet).

Coat metal with tempera paint.

Trace design onto metal.

Jewelry

This jewelry section assumes that anyone attempting this sort of project already has some skill in the handling of the necessary tools. It is also necessary to know something about etching and the chemicals involved. Nitric acid, used in this project, can cause physical harm if used without precautions and knowledge of its properties. Children certainly would need to be supervised in jewelry making by an experienced adult.

Small patterns or details from rubbings are most suitable as motifs for jewelry. A simple method for transferring the design is to coat a piece of metal with light-colored tempera paint. Then, when the paint has dried, tape a piece of carbon paper over the metal and tape the design you want to trace over this. Use a scribe, or a sharp pointed tool, and trace your lines into the metal so that the design remains after the tempera is washed away.

Cut the metal with a jeweler's saw. The metal should be placed in a bench clamp on a V block for working purposes. File the edges and smooth after you cut it. Abrasive cloths or papers may be used to remove scratch marks from metal surfaces. The piece to start with, as a first project, should not require soldering or etching. Small elements can have holes drilled in them and be hung as pendants.

The bracelet shown here was made of brass. Before shaping the bracelet, the rubbing design was etched into the metal, using the intaglio method: After cleaning the metal of all dirt and grease, both sides are coated, where needed, with black liquid asphaltum. Where there is no asphaltum, the acid "bites" the metal. The asphaltum protects the coated parts from the action of the acid, thus creating the design. When the asphaltum is dry, finer lines can be scratched into it with a burin. The metal is then immersed in a solution of nitric acid diluted with water. The more concentrated the nitric acid is, the faster the metal will be "bitten." After a few minutes, the metal is tested to see how deep the depressions are. When satisfied, the metal is rinsed with water and then cleaned with turpentine. It is now ready for shaping and polishing. You can use an oxidizing agent on the etched areas to emphasize the contrasts.

The bracelet was shaped by placing it over a mandrel and beating it with a rawhide mallet to form the curve.

The necklace was made in a way similar to that of the bracelet. Stamping and chasing tools may be used to bring out the designs into bas-relief. This is called chasing or repoussé. Enameling or cloisonné could also be used to point up the design.

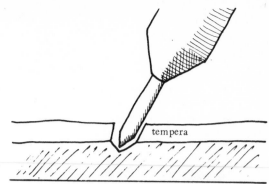
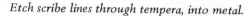

Etch scribe lines through tempera, into metal.

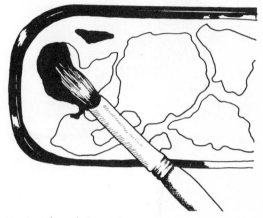

Coat with asphaltum those areas you do not want "bitten" by acid.

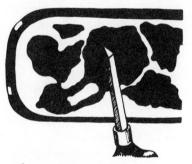

When asphaltum dries, etch in finer lines with a burin.

Immerse metal in acid solution.

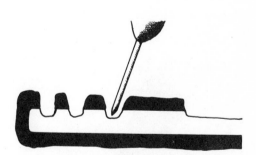

Test metal for depth of depressions.

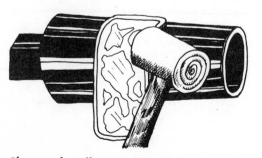

Shape with mallet over a mandrel.

Stamping and chasing tools.

Draw grid lines on muslin.

Pin along grain lines on garment.

Rub-offs

"Rub-offs," a most serviceable use for rubbings, were explained to me by a professor of fashion design at New York's Fashion Institute of Technology. They are rubbings done on garments for the purpose of duplicating the pattern. So-called line-for-line copies of European designer clothes are replicated in this way. It is less complicated to do a rub-off than to take a garment apart to copy it. By doing a rub-off you need not get involved with linings, interlinings, and facings, and the original item of clothing can be returned intact if it doesn't belong to you.

You might want to duplicate a garment in this way if you have some piece of clothing that fits you especially well and you want it in additional colors or fabrics, or if a worn-out item is no longer manufactured and you want to make a replacement or have one made for you.

The first step in producing a new pattern via the rub-off is to draw a grid (grain lines) on a section of muslin. To determine the yardage of muslin needed, measure a section of the garment at a time. For example, measure the length from the shoulder of the garment to the waist, on one side, and the width from the side seam to where the garment closes in front. Then cut a rectangle of muslin three or four inches larger than these measurements. Draw the grid lines on this piece of muslin with a ruler. The more intricate the design, the smaller the grid. In this illustration, the boxes are about four inches apart. Generally the grid lines are between two and four inches apart.

Next, use straight pins to indicate the fabric grain lines (grid) of the garment itself, in this same shoulder-to-waist area. Develop the length- and cross-grains by pinning a four-inch grid, like that of the muslin, on a flat portion of the garment. Following the grain of the fabric faithfully will reflect the contours of the garment (i.e., the four-inch grid will narrow around the waist and darts).

Next, line up the grid on the muslin with the pins on the garment. At this point, cut off the excess fabric around the armholes to make the muslin less cumbersome to work with. Pin muslin to garment. When the muslin and pins are aligned, the extra fabric forms the darts. You feel, as in Braille, where you know the darts to be. Use X's to mark the darts with colored pencil. Feel for the top and bottom of the dart and pin it in between on the muslin.

You are now ready to rub. Select a piece of colored wax tailor's crayon (not the chalk, which is white) and scrape it with a scissors so you have a sharp edge to work with. Then run this crayon along the muslin over seams, pockets, and buttons. If you insert pins along the seams, you will obtain an even clearer rubbing.

This entire process does not need to be executed on a mannequin—it can be done flat, laid out on a table. After completing the

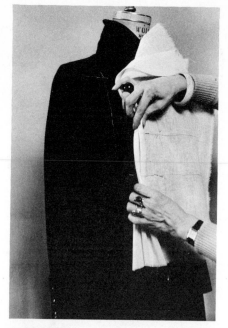

Line up grid on muslin with pins on garment.

Pin muslin to garment.

Gather extra muslin to form darts.

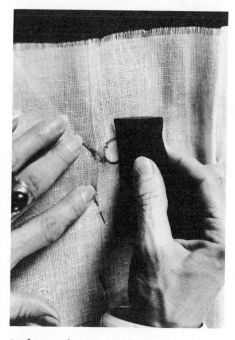

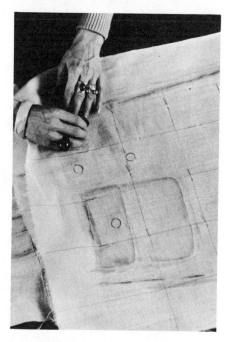

With pins along seams, begin to rub garment.

Garment may be removed from mannequin for rub-off.

Remove pattern from garment for cutting.

rub-off, remove the muslin from the garment and "true" your pattern by using a ruler to straighten out the straight lines and a French curve where necessary to follow the curves.

When cutting out the pattern with a scissors, allow ¼"-½" for seams. Continue this process around the garment until you have completed the pattern.

Retain a library or file of your patterns by folding them into appropriately marked envelopes.

Combined wax and graphite rubbing of found objects.

Rubbings of Your Own Design

It is interesting to make rubbings from your own designs. You can create original rubbings from the designs on etching plates, linoleum blocks, or woodcuts that you have produced yourself.

You can also build up designs from layers of cardboard. This creative technique has strong appeal for children: they can paste string, textured fabrics, doilies, veiling, and shapes cut out of cardboard onto a background of heavy paper board. The project can then be coated with Liquitex Gel to make it even and waterproof. When dry, tape it to a flat surface, tape rubbing paper over it, and rub. Rubbings can be monochromatic or multicolored. Fluorescent crayons may be used for variety. Colored wax-based pencils and China markers are also fun to use.

The children could do their rubbings directly onto a piece of fabric. Coins, fall leaves, or other "found objects" could be rubbed directly onto a shirt or scarf or cloth napkin. These would make unique gifts for family. Small objects do tend to slip around, so a small piece of double-faced tape should be placed underneath these items before proceeding to rub them. A little daub of clay or plasticine would also suffice.

A design may be "set" into the fabric by placing a damp towel over the wax design and pressing it with a warm iron. This should seal the wax enough to last through repeated washings. Fabrics containing some synthetic "hold" the wax better.

Wall Hanging or Banner

Victorian stones and ironwork are ideal resources for designs. They often have stylized patterns and flower arrangements which can be easily adapted to crafts projects. The wall hanging shown here is an interpretation of a carving.

I used felt for the background as well as for the leaf and floral details in the foreground. For variation, other kinds of fabric can be incorporated into your design. If you are doing a large wall hanging it will prove less expensive to use decorative burlap, which comes in a large variety of colors, for the background. Most of the supplies for this project can be purchased in a notions store or in the sewing section of a department store.

Wax rubbing from Victorian tombstone.

(Left): Cut out pattern paper, place on background fabric, and trace around it with pencil.

(Right): Trace outlines of design segments onto the different-colored felt pieces.

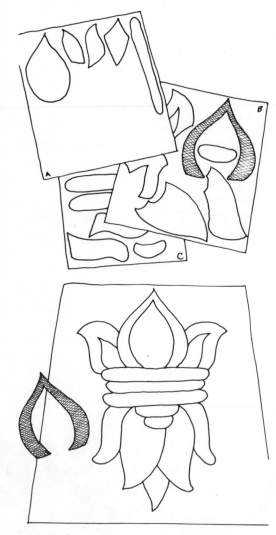

Cut out shapes traced on felt. Position, then glue shapes onto background material, which has been traced previously with entire design.

The first step is to press your background fabric to free it of wrinkles. Next, place it on a large flat surface, and use dress-pattern paper to trace the general outline of the rubbing (in other words. trace a silhouette of the pattern). Then cut out the pattern paper and place it exactly where you want it on the background fabric and trace around it with a pencil. Remove the pattern.

The next step is a little more complex, and if this is your first project, you should use a simple design. Put the original rubbing on a drawing board or any other flat surface and trace the rubbing, a section at a time: Select the color felt you want for the elements of your design, and place them in the correct location under the rubbing. Put a piece of dressmaker's carbon over the felt and beneath the rubbing, with the carbon side of the paper down. Use white carbon paper on dark colors and a dark-colored carbon paper on light colors. Use a dressmaker's tracing wheel to trace around each part of the design in order to transfer the markings to the felt. When you have done a few elements, remove the felt and position pieces of cut-out felt on the background. If you feel it would be helpful you can completely trace your rubbing onto the background with the carbon paper and tracing wheel and then have less guessing as to where each piece goes. Do not attach the pieces permanently until they are all cut out. In order not to lose the pieces during this interim, you can carefully place a piece of glass over them. This way they will not be blown away and you can leave the project in an unobtrusive place for days before returning to it.

When all the pieces are cut out and properly positioned, paste them down with white glue like Sobo or Elmer's. You can apply these glues with a small, flat paintbrush or with your fingers. Some bottles have dispenser tips. Use enough glue to generously cover the back of the piece to be pasted down to within a quarter-inch of its edge. Carefully place the piece into position, pressing the edges firmly to the background. Water can be used to remove any excess glue and to clean your brushes. Adhesive spray may be used—follow directions on the can.

You may decide to embroider certain sections or use waterproof felt-tip markers to emphasize details.

When all the pieces have been pasted in place your wall hanging is complete except for the hangers. Loops can be made of the same or contrasting felt and attached to the background fabric, or you can purchase plastic strips which slip onto the edges of the felt. The top hanger usually has a cord attached.

The other mounting possibility is to stretch the hanging over a framework ordinarily used for oil painting canvases. Decorative fringe or tassels can then be hung from the bottom for a still more finished look.

Paper Collage

A rubbing can be easily traced and used as the pattern for a collage. Both paper and fabric collages are especially suitable projects for children. The procedure for paper collage is simpler. Select background paper, trace shapes with tracing paper. Use all kinds of papers for the decorative elements: foreign newspapers, wallpapers, doilies, foils, and imported papers—the choice is almost infinite. Prepasted papers are available for use by younger children. Cut out tracing paper and decorative elements simultaneously. Be sure to use sharp scissors. Embroidery or cuticle scissors are invaluable for intricate shapes. Hole punchers can be used to obtain small round circles. Discard the tracing paper and arrange the decorative elements on background paper. Glue with white glue or spray adhesive. Weight the collage so that it will dry flat.

Art Deco graphite rubbing; Bronx County Courthouse.

Iron-ons

Wax rubbing from tombstone.

Designs from rubbings can also be translated into fabric collages such as wall hangings or banners. These simply carry the basic techniques of paper collage into another medium. Many types of cloth may be used in their construction, but most notable are the special fabrics manufactured for repair purposes, like iron-on patches. These fabrics become bonded to the fabric they are ironed onto. For our purposes, rubbings can be traced onto this fabric and employed in a fabric collage or appliqué. Embroidery or fabric painting can also be incorporated into this process. Some manufacturers have produced decorative pieces and initials from this fabric, which can be ironed on and included in your design. Decide on an item you wish to make and cut out your fabric accordingly. Lightly outline your design on the background material with dressmaker's wax or chalk. You can use the same tracing procedures described in the section on wall hangings. I used a dark background for this iron-on, and therefore used white dressmaker's carbon paper to transfer the tracing.

Press background fabric before cutting out iron-on shapes. To bond the iron-on pieces to the background, use a dry iron—do not use steam. Regulate your iron dial by pointing the setting arrow to "wool." Iron the area on the fabric to be "patched" and then apply the cutout, shiny side down. Hold your iron down firmly on the cutout for about thirty seconds. Don't slide the iron across the area. If you are ironing on a large cutout, do it in sections at a time, pressing down on each section for about thirty seconds. Press around the edges of the iron-on to complete the seal. Manufacturers suggest laundering your background material prior to the iron-on process. After you have finished your design, complete any necessary sewing. My iron-on was to be made into a pillow, so I simply cut out an equal size piece of fabric, sewed up three sides, stuffed it with a foam pillow form, and sewed it closed.

Stained Glass

Rubbings can be very useful in the art of stained glass. Not only can original designs made from them be translated into stained-glass ornaments, but craftspeople who specialize in the repair of leaded glass employ them to make patterns of damaged parts. A precise pattern can be copied from an original piece via a graphite rubbing, which can be done using very little pressure. This technique is also utilized for reproducing perfect replicas of manufactured patterns. Tiffany patterns are sometimes pirated in this manner.

The following equipment is needed to make a leaded-glass piece: a glass cutter, ruler, scissors, adjustable pliers, cardboard or paper for patterns, solder, soldering iron (preferably with a stainless-steel tip, which makes clean-up minimal), flux or tinner's solution, copper foil tape, and U- or H-shaped lead.

To produce an original stained-glass piece from a rubbing it is best to make two rubbings of the design you wish to reproduce. The first rubbing is used as your pattern and the second to lay out your cut-out glass pieces on.

A rubbing from a heat register in the Petit Memorial Library in Wilmington, Vermont was the model for this stained-glass window. Inasmuch as the pattern had many small pieces, some liberties were taken with the design, incorporating some of the smaller pieces to make larger ones.

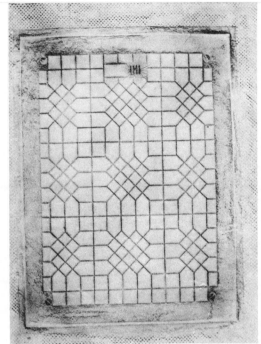

Graphite rubbing from floor heat-register; Library, Wilmington, Vt.

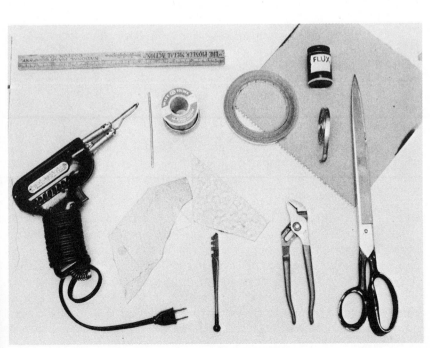

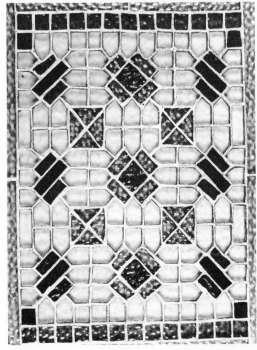

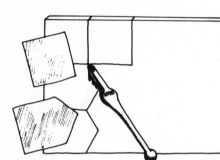

Using cut-up rubbing as pattern, trace outlines on glass with a grease pencil, then score them with glass cutter.

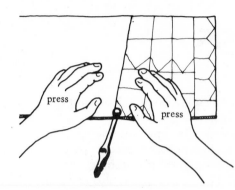

Break glass along score lines.

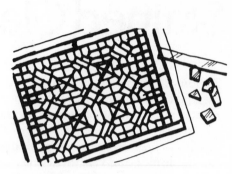

Lay cut pieces on extra rubbing.

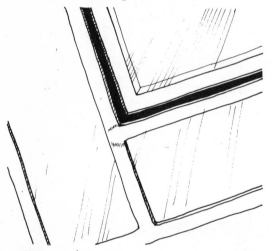

Leading.

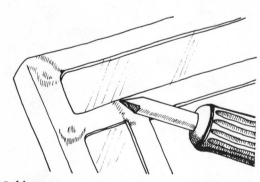

Soldering.

It is easiest to cut up one of the rubbings and place each piece on the glass. Then you can cut around the pattern. It is also possible to do the reverse if the glass is transparent enough. Place the pattern under the glass and then trace the outline of the piece to be cut with a grease pencil. Cut on this line with the glass cutter. When working with large numbers of glass pieces it is necessary to allow 1/16" to 1/8" for the width of the lead. Professionals use double-bladed knives for this purpose.

Glass to be cut should be placed on a flat, resilient surface and the cutter run on the line only one time. A light scoring is all that is necessary. To break the glass along the cut, the lower end of the glass is lifted and the handle of the glass cutter is placed under the score line. Then about ten pounds of downward pressure is applied manually on either side of this line and the glass breaks clean. It is often helpful to tap the bottom side of the glass along the path of the score to facilitate separating it.

For best results when making the score lines the cutter must be in good condition. Cutting will be much simpler if you keep it submerged in light oil or kerosene when it is not in use. The lubricant reduces heat and friction along the cutting line, therefore assuring a cleaner cut.

As the pieces are cut, position them on the second rubbing. Once all the pieces are cut out they are put together with lead and soldering. This process is called glazing. The longer the pieces of lead used, the fewer the number of joints to be soldered. The lead should be firmly pressed onto the edges of the glass so that no light shows between the glass and the lead. Joints should not be melted by keeping the soldering iron on them too long.

Greeting Cards

Stationery and cards are a "natural" for rubbings. The rubbings can be done directly onto ready-made cards or stationery. Blank greeting cards are sold in art-supply stores complete with matching envelopes. Rubbings can also be enlarged, reduced, and reproduced through the photostatic process and pasted onto various sized papers. You can even Xerox your rubbing designs. Elegant looking cards can be made from photostated rubbing designs and reproduced, in quantity, by a professional printer, messages and names printed inside at the same time.

The cards shown here were produced by photostatically reducing the rubbings to the sizes desired and then mounting them on fine stock paper. These rubbings were taken from the ark doors on the altar of the Central Synagogue.

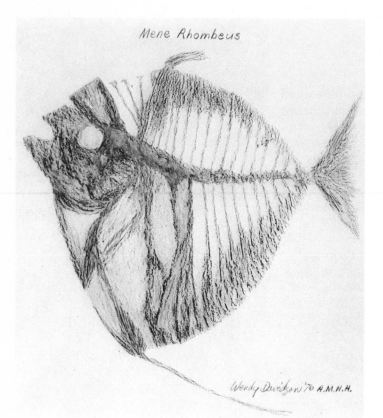

Mene Rhombeus

Wendy Davidson '70 A.M.N.H.

Decorative Sketches

Due to their generally delicate quality, certain shells and fossils lend themselves to attractive decorative handling. If possible to do so, it is less cumbersome to make casts of plaster of the objects you wish to rub and then use flexible lead wax-based pencils for the rubbing. The fish-fossil rubbing shown here is from a cast made in the reproduction department of the American Museum of Natural History. The pencils used were Eagle Prismacolor—heavy crayons are not appropriate for such delicate rubbings. The fish was rubbed on tracing tissue with the colored pencils. A watercolor wash, for decorative purposes, was then applied over the waxy pencil. The paint "resists" the wax so the lines are therefore not obliterated.

The nautilus shell was done directly from the shell with China marking pencils, Prismacolors, and a watercolor wash on architectural detail paper.

Woven Art

An interesting interpretation of an Art Deco border was carried out on a four-harness table loom with a double weave. It is assumed that the person attempting such a project is a weaver of some experience.

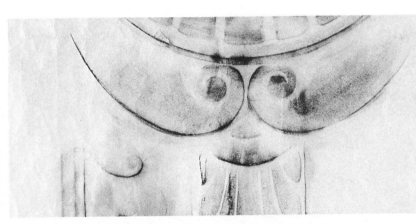

Graphite rubbing taken from motif on Bronx County Courthouse.

Twelve threads were used to the inch for this weaving. Lily Mills Company 3/2 Pearl cotton was employed.

Other Possibilities

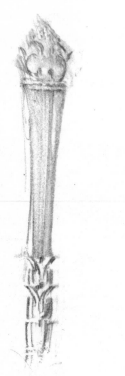

Rubbings also have practical purposes, as noted in the section on rub-offs. It is safer to carry around a rubbing of your favorite silver pattern to match it up than to carry the piece of silver with you. You can do a rubbing of a piece of jewelry to illustrate it to another person.

A rubbing of an old furniture label is often more legible than the label itself. Museum curators, to verify authenticity, sometimes rub an object to see details they may miss with the naked eye.

Why carry a whole floor tile to the floor-covering store—just take a rubbing.

Craft shops and craft magazines are endless sources for inspiration as to what next you can create from your rubbings. Tooling foil, mosaics, tissue paper, wire, batik, liquid metal, cork, are all adaptable. The possibilities are only limited by your imagination . . . and the strong Aqaba paper you thought you ruined with a poor rubbing can be used to make a good paper kite!

Label from old piece of furniture.

Floor tile.

Bibliography

Rubbing Techniques

Andrew, Laye. *Creative Rubbings.* New York: Watson-Guptill Publications, 1967.

Bertram, Jerome. *Brasses and Brass Rubbing in England.* Devon, U.K.: David and Charles, 1971.

Bodor, Jolin J. *Rubbings and Textures: A Graphic Technique.* New York: Reinhold Book Corp., 1968.

Busby, Richard J. *Beginner's Guide to Brass Rubbing.* London: Pelham Books, 1971.

Cook, Malcolm. *Discovering Brasses and Brass Rubbing.* Hertsforshire, Eng.: Shire Publications, 1970.

Eppink, Norman R. *101 Prints: The History and Technique of Printmaking.* Norman, Okla.: University of Oklahoma Press, 1971

Firestein, Cecily Barth. "Rubbing History and Nostalgia in the Bronx." *Bronx County Historical Journal.* Volume 13 No. 2, Fall 1976, Bronx, New York, Bronx County Historical Society.

Friede, E.P. "Rubbings from Rock Engravings (Discussion of a recent method)." *Africana Notes and News,* Vol. 11, No. 6 (March 1955), Africana Museum, City of Johannesburg.

Gillon, Edmund V., Jr. *Early New England Gravestone Rubbings.* New York: Dover Publications, 1966.

Hirsch, Bob. "Hang that Memory." *Relax,* March 1973.

Hiyama, Yoshio. *Gyotaku: The Art and Technique of the Japanese Fish Print.* Seattle: University of Washington Press, 1964.

Marks, Glen K. *Oldstone's Guide to Creative Rubbing.* Boston: Oldstone Enterprises, 1973.

Pluckrose, Henry. *Introducing Crayon Techniques.* New York: Watson-Guptill Publications, 1967.

Skinner, Michael K. *How to Make Rubbings.* New York: Van Nostrand Reinhold, Studio Vista, 1972.

Description of Brasses, Gravestones, and Rubbings

Clayton, Muriel M.A. *Catalogue of Rubbings of Brasses and Incised Slabs.* London: Her Majesty's Stationery Office, 1968.

De Sala Paol, David. *Portraits Etched in Stone: Early Jewish Settlers, 1682-1831.* New York: Columbia University Press, 1952.

Forbes, Harriette M. *Gravestones of Early New England and the Men Who Made Them, 1653-1800.* Princeton, N.J.: The Pyne Press, 1955.

Jacobs, G. Walker. *Stranger Stop and Cast an Eye: A Guide to Stones and Rubbings.* Marblehead, Mass.: Oldstone Enterprises, 1972.

Ludwig, Allan I. *Graven Images: New England Stone Carving and Its Symbols, 1650-1815.* Middletown, Conn.: Weslyan University Press, 1966.

Morris, Malcolm. *Brass Rubbing.* New York: Dover Publications, 1965.

Patter, Gail M. *Stories Behind the Stones.* Cranbury, N.J.: A.S. Barney & Co., 1969.

Smith, Elmer L. *Early American Gravestone Designs.* Lebanon, Pa.: Applied Arts Publishers, 1972.

Tashjian, Ann, and Tashjian, Dickran. *Memorials for Children of Change: The Art of Early New England Stonecarving.* Middletown, Conn.: Weslyan University Press, 1974.

Trinick, Henry. *The Craft and Design of Monumental Brasses.* New York: The Humanities Press, 1969.

Wasserman, Emily. *Gravestone Designs.* New York: Dover Publications, 1972.

Williams, Melvin G. *The Last Word: The Lure and Lore of Early New England Graveyards.* Boston, Mass.: Oldstone Enterprises, 1973.

Wust, Kalus. *Folk Art in Stone.* Edinburg, Va.: West Virginia Shenandoah History, 1970.

Related Crafts

Ackley, Edith F. *Dolls to Make for Fun and Profit.* New York: Frederick A. Stokes Co., 1938.

Biegeleisen, J.I., and Cohn, Max Arthur. *Silk Screen Techniques.* New York: Dover Publications, 1958.

Biegeleisen, J.I. *Silk Screen Craft as a Hobby.* New York: Harper & Bros., 1939.

Blumenau, Lili. *The Art and Craft of Handweaving.* New York: Crown Publishers, 1971.

Brigadier, Anne. *Collage: A Complete Guide for Artists.* New York: Watson-Guptill Publications, 1970.

Corbin, Thomas J. *Hand Block Printing on Fabrics.* London: Sir Issac Pitman & Sons, 1934.

Freehof, L., and Kind, B. *Embroideries and Fabrics for Synagogue and Home.* Great Neck, N.Y.: Hearthside Press, 1966.

Goldman, Phyllis. *Make It From Felt.* New York: Funk & Wagnalls, 1974.

Gray, Ilse. *Designing and Making Dolls.* New York: Watson-Guptill Publications, 1972.

Heller, Jules. *Printmaking Today.* New York: Holt, Rinehart and Winston, 1972.

Instruction Manual, Screen Printing. Slatesville, N.C.: Speedball-Hunt Manufacturing Co., Current.

Lawless, Dorothy. *Rug Hooking and Braiding for Pleasure and Profit.* New York: Thomas Y. Crowell Co., 1962.

Lindemeyer, Nancy; Vaughan, Ciba; and Johnston, Rebecca. "Designs from Rubbings." *Better Homes and Gardens,* August 1975.

Luciano. *Stained Glass Window Art.* New York: Hidden House/Flash Books, 1974.

Mendez, Pepe. *Complete Course in Stained Glass.* New York: Quick Fox, 1977.

One Hundred Embroidery Stitches. Book no. 150-A. New York: Coats and Clark, 1975.

Raymo, Anne, and Vose, Holly. *Sew-Up Art: Appliqué—How To Do It.* New York: Quick Fox, 1976.

Rockland, Mae S. *The Work of Our Hands.* New York: Schocken Books, 1973.

Rathenstein, Michael. *Linocuts and Woodcuts.* New York: Watson-Guptill Publications, 1967.

Sommer, Elyse, and Sommer, Mike. *A New Look at Felt.* New York: Crown Publishers, 1975.

Sunset Books, and *Sunset Magazine,* editors of. *Needlepoint.* Menlo Park, Cal.: Lane Books, 1975.

Sunset Books. *Stitchery (Embroidery, Appliqué, Crewel).* Menlo Park, Cal.: Lane Books, 1974.

Statton, Charlotte K. *Rug Hooking Made Easy.* New York: Harper & Row, 1975.

Vanderbilt, Gloria. *Collage.* New York: Galahad Books, 1970.

Van Tassel, Raymond. *Woodworking Crafts.* New York: D. Van Nostrand Co., 1951.

Wiener, Louis. *Hand-Made Jewelry.* New York: D. Van Nostrand Co., 1948.

Wilson, Erica. *Embroidery Book.* New York: Charles Scribner's Sons, 1973.

Wiseman, Ann. *Rags, Rugs and Wool Pictures: A First Book of Rug Hooking.* New York: Charles Scribner's Sons, 1968.

Related Reference Literature

Deetz, James F., and Dethlefsen, Edwin S. "Death's Head, Urn and Willow." In *Contemporary Archaeology,* edited by Mark P. Leone, Chapter 33. Carbondale, Ill: Southern Illinois University Press, 1972.

Hardgrove, Regina C., and Fairbanks, Elaine C. *Epitaphs from Halifax, Vermont.* Brattleboro, Vt.: John B. Fowler, 1973.

Laver, James. *Costume.* New York: Hawthorne Books, 1963.

Mann, Thomas C., and Greene, Janet. *Over Their Dead Bodies: Yankee Epitaphs and History.* Brattleboro, Vt.: The Stephen Greene Press, 1962.

Mann, Thomas C., and Greene, Janet. *Sudden and Awful: American Epitaphs and the Finger of God.* Brattleboro, Vt.: The Stephen Greene Press, 1968.

Martin, Henry C. *Comic Epitaphs: From the Very Best 'Old Graveyards.* Mt. Vernon, N.Y.: Peter Pauper Press, 1957.

Ting Chou Fong. *Stone Rubbings.* Falls Church, Va.: Cathay House (a commercial catalogue), current.

Architectural Guides to Rubbing Sites

Gayle, Margot, and Gillon Edmund V., Jr. *Cast Iron Architecture in New York: A Photographic Survey.* New York: Dover Publications, 1974.

Hallander, Anne. "Art Deco's Back and New York's Got It." *New York Magazine,* November 11, 1974.

Huxtable, Ada L. *Classic New York: Georgian Gentility to Greek Elegance.* Garden City, N.Y.: Doubleday Anchor Books, 1964.

Jacoby, Stephen J. *Architectural Sculpture in New York City.* New York: Dover Publications, 1975.

Sullivan, Donald, and Danforth, Brian. *Bronx Art Deco Architecture (An Exposition).* New York: Publishing Center for Cultural Resources (Copyright, Hunter College Graduate Program in Urban Planning), 1976.

Vlack, Don. *Art Deco Architecture in New York, 1920-1940.* New York: Harper & Row, 1974.

White, Norval, and Wilensky, Elliott. *A I A Guide to New York City.* New York: The Macmillian Co., 1967.

Guide Books for Rubbing Sites and Landmarks in New York City

Butler, John V. *Churchyards of Trinity Parish in the City of New York: 1697-1969.* New York: Corporation of Trinity Church, 1969.

Fried, Frederick, and the Brooklyn Museum. *Fragmentary Landmarks: Sculpture Gardens, Brooklyn Museum.* New York: The Brooklyn Museum Press, 1966.

Gladstone, Harmon H., and Dalrymple, Martin. *History Preserved: A Guide to New York City Landmarks and Historic Districts.* New York: Simon & Schuster, 1974.

Hall, Edward H. *A Guide to the Cathedral Church of Saint John the Divine in the City of New York.* New York: The Dean and Chapter of the Cathedral Church, 1965.

New York Community Trust. *The Heritage of New York: Historic Landmark Plaques of the New York Community Trust.* New York: Fordham University Press, 1970.

Richmond, John, and Lamarque, Abril. *Brooklyn, U.S.A.* New York: Creative Age Press, 1946.

Robinson, Cervin, and Bletter, Rosemarie H. *Skyscraper Style: Art Deco New York.* New York: Oxford Book Co., Inc. 1975.

Shaw, Charles G. *New York—Oddly Enough.* New York: Farrar and Rinehart, 1938.

Stone, Elaine, and Harris, Phyllis. "A Walking Tour of Central Synagogue" (illustrated with rubbings by Cecily Firestein). New York: *Central Synagogue Handbook,* 1976-77.

Streeter, Edward. *The Story of the Woodlawn Cemetery.* New York: The Woodlawn Cemetery, current.

Ullman, Albert. *A Landmark History of New York.* New York: D. Appleton-Century Co., 1939.

Index

Acrylic paint, 37, 56, 60, 70
Aluminum foil, 42
Angkor Wat, 5
Appliqué, 62-63
Aqaba paper, 21
Archaeology, 5, 15
Architecture, 5, 7, 10, 51
Art Deco, 11, 52, 91
Asphaltum, 79

Banners: see Wall hangings
Beeswax: see Wax
Blocking, 70-71
Block printing, 52-55, 85; see also Linocuts
Bokutaku (Sumi rubbing), 25
Brass, 14-15; see also Monumental brasses
Brushes, 25, 27
Burnisher, 42
Burnishing, 55

Canvas, 70-71
Carbon paper, 38-39, 52; see also Dress-
    maker's carbon
Cardboard, 27, 82
Cathedral of St. John the Divine (N.Y.), 65
Central Synagogue (N.Y.), 44
Chasing, 79
Collage, 85
Crayons, 22-24
Cutouts, 56-59

Dabbing, 31, 36-37
Display, 44-46
Dolls, 68-69
Dressmaker's carbon, 65, 66, 84
Dry mounting, 45

Electric pen, 60-61
Embroidery, 64-67; hand, 64-65;
    machine, 66-67
Embroidery hoop, 65, 66, 67
Etching, 78-79

Fabrics, 22, 68, 80, 83-84, 86
Felt, 84
Fish rubbing: see Gyotaku
Fixative, 31
Fossils, 16, 90

Gesso, 59
Glass, 87-88; see also Leaded glass;
    Stained glass
Glazing, 88
Gold leaf, 60-61
Gouge, 53-54
Graphite, 24, 29-31
Graphite paste, 24, 29-31, 37
Gravestones, 14, 16-17, 56, 62-63
Greeting cards, 89
Gyotaku, 14, 20, 44

Heel ball, 23

India ink, 23
Inks, 24-25, 53
Ironing, 36, 46, 67, 86
Iron-ons, 77, 86

Jewelry, 78-79
Jio-ta-ku, 20

Kneepads, 25

Lampblack, 23
Landmarks, 10, 44
Latch hooking, 72-73
Leaded glass, 87-88
Lifting, 27-29
Linocuts, 52-56
Linoleum blocks, 52-54
Loom, 91

Matrix, 77
Molds, 42
Monumental brasses, 14-15
Museums, 5, 15-16, 70, 90
Muslin, 80-81

Needlepoint, 70-71
Nitric acid, 78-79

Oils, 24

Paper, 20-22
Permission and permits, 20
Photographic transfer, 77
Photostats, 70, 89

Pillows, 68-69
Plaster of paris, 42
Positive impression, 29

Renk ink, 24
Reproduction, 44
Rice paper, 20
Rubbing, history of, 14-17
Rubbing techniques, 20, 26-39, 42;
    carbon-paper, 20, 38-39; dry, 20, 26-32;
    foil, 20, 42; wet, 20, 33-37
Rub-off, 80-81

Scribe, 78
Sewing machine, 66-67
Shells, 90
Shrink wrapping, 45
Silkscreens, 74-76
Soldering, 87-88
Sprayer, 25
Stained glass, 87-88
Stencils, 74-76
Stippling, 61
Stitches, 65-67; see also Needlepoint
Sumi ink, 14, 24-25, 37
Suppliers, 46-49; mail-order, 47-49

Tailor's crayon, 80
Tape, 27, 28
T'a-pen, 14
Tracing, 52, 65
Tracing paper, 21
Tracing wheel, 84
T-shirt, 77

Varnish and shellac, 61
Victoria and Albert Museum, 16

Wall hangings, 83-84
Wax, 22-24, 62
Weaving, 91
Woodburning, 60-61
Wood carving, 61
Woodworking, 56-61

Yarn, 70